The Hundred Years' War

An Enthralling Guide to the Epic Struggle for Dominance Between England and France

© Copyright 2025 - All rights reserved.

The content contained within this book may not be reproduced, duplicated, or transmitted without direct written permission from the author or the publisher.

Under no circumstances will any blame or legal responsibility be held against the publisher, or author, for any damages, reparation, or monetary loss due to the information contained within this book, either directly or indirectly.

Legal Notice:

This book is copyright protected. It is only for personal use. You cannot amend, distribute, sell, use, quote, or paraphrase any part, or the content within this book, without the consent of the author or publisher.

Disclaimer Notice:

Please note the information contained within this document is for educational and entertainment purposes only. All effort has been executed to present accurate, up-to-date, reliable, and complete information. No warranties of any kind are declared or implied. Readers acknowledge that the author is not engaging in the rendering of legal, financial, medical, or professional advice. The content within this book has been derived from various sources. Please consult a licensed professional before attempting any techniques outlined in this book.

By reading this document, the reader agrees that under no circumstances is the author responsible for any losses, direct or indirect, that are incurred as a result of the use of the information contained within this document, including, but not limited to, errors, omissions, or inaccuracies.

Free limited time bonus

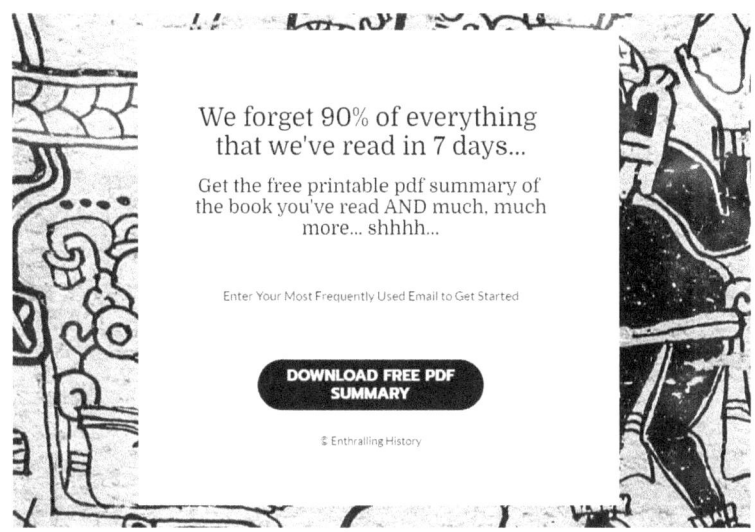

Stop for a moment. We have a free bonus set up for you. The problem is this: we forget 90% of everything that we read after 7 days. Crazy fact, right? Here's the solution: we've created a printable, 1-page pdf summary for this book that you're reading now. All you have to do to get your free pdf summary is to go to the following website: https://livetolearn.lpages.co/enthrallinghistory/

Or, Scan the QR code!

Once you do, it will be intuitive. Enjoy, and thank you!

Table of Contents

INTRODUCTION 1
CHAPTER 1: THE BEGINNING 3
CHAPTER 2: THE BATTLES OF SLUYS AND CRÉCY 12
CHAPTER 3: THE BLACK DEATH AND THE BLACK PRINCE 21
CHAPTER 4: THE ART OF WAR 30
CHAPTER 5: SOCIETY IN CHAOS 38
CHAPTER 6: THE TREATY OF BRÉTIGNY 49
CHAPTER 7: HENRY, AGINCOURT, AND JOAN 59
CHAPTER 8: CULTURE OF THE HUNDRED YEARS' WAR 73
CHAPTER 9: THE COLLAPSE OF ENGLISH POWER 82
CHAPTER 10: THE END OF THE FIGHTING 96
CHAPTER 11: THE LEGACY 102
CONCLUSION 110
HERE'S ANOTHER BOOK BY ENTHRALLING HISTORY THAT YOU MIGHT LIKE 112
FREE LIMITED TIME BONUS 113
BIBLIOGRAPHY 114
IMAGE SOURCES 121

Introduction

England and France were in a state of war from 1337 to 1453. It is known as the Hundred Years' War, and although it was not a continuous conflict, the war created anarchy and violence that generated suffering on a grand scale. Treaties were made and then broken, alliances were formed and collapsed, and armed warfare dominated the policy decisions of the two nations. England was ruled by the Plantagenet dynasty at the beginning and the House of Lancaster at the end. France was governed by the House of Valois for the entirety of the Hundred Years' War.

Society morphed in both countries. Feudal relationships that had once been the heart of the medieval social order gave way to centralized states in which the Crown, not the local lord, was the authority. France developed a national identity, something it had not enjoyed for centuries. The terror and deaths caused by the Black Death also affected England and France, creating social upheaval. England would have to endure the Peasants' Revolt. People looked up to heroes such as Joan of Arc and King Henry V.

The Hundred Years' War was more than arrows and swords. Culture continued to develop, and literary works such as *The Canterbury Tales* were being produced. Oxford and the University of Paris had vigorous debates on philosophy and science, and scholars like John Wycliffe posed questions that disturbed the established order. One of the most significant changes of this period was that English became the primary language in England. Henry IV was the first monarch to officially speak English instead of French.

Battles and politics are, of course, essential to any discussion about the Hundred Years' War, but the progress of English and French societies merits consideration as well. Medieval feudalism gradually disappeared during this period, and the ideas and mindset of the Renaissance started to appear. By the end of this book, you will understand that the Hundred Years' War was more than just knights in shining armor brawling on muddy battlefields.

One note before we start. Throughout the book, there are references to Aquitaine, Guyenne, and Gascony. These all refer to the southwest region of France, which was either all or in part owned by England for approximately three hundred years.

Chapter 1: The Beginning

Family was very important in medieval Europe. A person who was an aristocrat or a royal owed allegiance more to their family name than to a nation. Marriages were highly political, and family ties instead of patriotism were often the most important considerations whenever a dispute arose. Bloodlines and nationalism played prominent roles at different stages in the longest war in European history.

The Hundred Years' War did not happen overnight. Historians argue about its origins, with some saying that the seeds of the conflict were sown as early as 1066 when William of Normandy conquered England. That victory by the Norman duke tied England to French territory. The Angevin Empire of the Plantagenets included England and nearly all eastern France. The French Crown gradually chipped away at the English possessions in France until all that was left was the Duchy of Gascony.

<u>The Succession Crisis</u>

The House of Capet began to be the ruling royal family of France in 987. In 1313, Philip IV died, leaving behind three sons. Ordinarily, there would be no succession problems, but all three died without a surviving male heir. The last, Charles IV, died in 1328. There were three possible heirs to the throne at that time.

- Philip, Count of Valois, was King Philip III's grandson and Philip IV's nephew.
- Joan II of Navarre was the daughter of King Louis X (r. 1314-1316) and an heir-general of Philip IV.

- Edward III of England was the son of Isabella of France, who was the only surviving child of Philip IV. Edward's claim rested on being a grandson of Philip IV.

An image of Edward III from the 16th century.[1]

Joan was disqualified because she was a woman; Salic Law did not allow a female to inherit the throne. While France did not allow a woman to be a monarch, English custom permitted succession through the female line. However, Edward was a minor at the time of the succession dispute. Isabella claimed the throne on his behalf, but that did not sit well with the French aristocracy.

The nobles of France did not want a foreigner to sit on the French throne, especially if that person was English. The lords of France chose

Philip, Count of Valois, to be the new king of France. He would reign as Philip VI. If Edward wanted to be the king of France, he would have to go to war. The young English monarch, though, was still under the control of his regents. He had to deal with his mother and her lover, Roger Mortimer. Any thought of backing up his claims with force would have to wait.

Establishing Royal Authority

Philip VI realized that he would have to assert his authority with a firm hand to keep his crown. His dynasty was new, and some would contest his legitimacy, especially if Philip proved to be a weak ruler. So, the new king hit the ground running.

Flanders was an important commercial center in the 14th century because it controlled the cloth industry. A rebellion broke out in 1328, and the count of Flanders appealed to Philip for assistance. The French king immediately sent help, and the rebellion was crushed at the Battle of Cassel. The victory allowed Philip to have effective suzerainty over Flanders. However, a serious internal problem followed that required action.[1]

Robert of Artois was a French noble who had been a supporter of Philip during the succession crisis. There was a dispute over the courtship of Artois that pitted Robert against a member of the royal family. Legal proceedings followed, and it was discovered that Robert had forged his late father's will, consequently voiding his claim to Artois. Robert did not respond to a summons to appear before the king and was sentenced in absentia to exile. He had his estates confiscated on April 8th, 1332. Robert eventually fled to England and was accepted by Edward and the English royal court. Robert was now a serious enemy of Philip VI, and he would encourage Edward III to actively contest for the French throne.

The Oath of Fealty

According to medieval tradition and custom, a noble who held land in a fief had to swear an oath of fealty, or loyalty, to his overlord. Edward III held territory in France (Aquitaine), so he had to go through that ceremony. Moreover, Philip VI expected Edward to do it.

---

[1] Britannica, E. o. (2024, June 29). *Philip VI*. Retrieved from Britannica.com: https://www.britannica.com/biography/Philip-VI

The ceremony happened at Amiens Cathedral on June 6th, 1329. It was not an ordinary oath-taking. The ceremony ordinarily would include an oath of fealty, but the previous kings of England, Edward I and Edward II, did not swear an oath of fealty during their visits. Likewise, Edward III only pledged a conditional homage without the oath of fidelity. Even though he was summoned in 1330 and again in 1331 to swear the required oath of fidelity, Edward never paid liege homage to Philip.[i]

The Auld Alliance

The oath of fidelity was not the only bone of contention between the two monarchs. France and Scotland entered an alliance in 1295 that required either country to come to the aid of the other if England attacked. That didn't stop England from attacking Scotland. Edward II's weak rule and the military genius of Robert the Bruce saved Scotland from being absorbed by England. So, no great sense of urgency was tied to this alliance until 1332.

Edward III wanted to establish his authority in both Scotland and France. The alliance now had a sense of urgency, and Philip sent military support and one thousand pounds to help the Scots. Both members of the alliance were willing to assist each other in keeping England restrained.

This posed a significant problem for Edward. He could not move against either country without being attacked from the rear. That possibility was going to affect his decisions in the coming years.

Trade and Commerce

Tensions between France and England started growing between 1332 and 1337. A source of animosity between the two countries at the time involved a bottle of claret.

Claret is a red wine produced from grapes in southwestern France, particularly Gascony, which was an English possession. England imported a large volume of Gascon wine, which was a source of revenue for the English Crown. Gascony was an essential part of the English

---

[i] University of California Press. (2024, June 29). *The Five Substitutions.* Retrieved from UC Press E-Books Collection, 1982-2004:
https://publishing.cdlib.org/ucpressebooks/view?docId=ft8k4008jd&chunk.id=d0e4248&toc.depth=1&toc.id=d0e4231&brand=ucpress#:~:text=When%20Philip%20of%20Valois%20came,fidelity%20to%20the%20French%20ruler

economy. Gascony needed products such as grain, wool, and dried fish, which were all provided by English merchants. England relied on salt from the salt pits of Bordeaux, and armor was another export from Gascony to England.[i]

The financial importance of Gascony was undeniable. The revenue extracted from the wine trade alone earned the English Crown more than all the revenue of England, Wales, and Ireland in 1327. Losing that possession would be a critical blow to English prosperity, and the French were very aware of that.[ii]

France used the threat of seizing that territory to curb any aggressive English policy. King Philip VI wanted this territory for economic and strategic reasons. The financial gain was obvious. France could assume the lucrative wine-exporting commerce, depriving Edward of badly needed revenue. Moreover, Gascony's location would permit Philip to exercise more influence in southern France.

Control of Flanders was another economic point of contention. The Low Countries were an essential cog in England's wheel of fortune. England was a significant exporter of wool, and Europe's cloth industry was centered in Flanders. Cities like Ghent, Bruges, and Ypres took bales of English wool and turned them into yards and yards of cloth. There had already been violent disturbances in Flanders, and England saw an opportunity to increase its influence by supporting the urban uprisings. The French were trying to offset that, creating a power play.

The location of Flanders made it strategically significant. Whoever had control of that region could also influence maritime trade in the English Channel and some very important trade routes in northern Europe.

The War Drums

England involved itself in the dynastic disputes occurring in Scotland. The Scottish king, Robert the Bruce, died in 1329 and was succeeded by his five-year-old son, David II. Edward Balliol, the son of an earlier monarch, John Balliol, invaded Scotland in 1332 to press his claim to the throne. He provoked a civil war in the process. Fortunately for

---

[i] Sargent, F. (2018). *The Wine Trade with Gascony.* Retrieved from British History Online: https://www.british-history.ac.uk/manchester-uni/london-lay-subsidy/1332/pp256-311

[ii] II, A. L. (2024, June 29). *Gascony and the Causes of the Hundred Years' War.* Retrieved from Medievalists.net: https://www.medievalists.net/2020/02/gascony-causes-of-the-hundred-years-war/

Balliol, he had the support of Edward III. Edward Balliol ultimately forced King David II of Scotland to flee to France. The French were deeply concerned about England's involvement in Scotland, which caused a strain in relations between England and France.[i]

What finally brought things to a head and started the war was feudal politics. Edward's behavior in Amiens Cathedral was never forgotten or forgiven. Edward was technically a vassal of Philip VI, and he was expected to pay homage to the French king. Philip concluded that Edward had been deficient in his duties as a vassal. Consequently, Philip believed that he had the right to confiscate English holdings in France. On May 24th, 1337, Philip VI formally declared that Edward had forfeited Aquitaine for failing to fulfill his duties. Philip included in his charges against Edward that the English king had granted asylum to Robert of Artois, whom Philip considered his mortal enemy. Philip declared that what Edward III was doing fit the protocols of a *bellum justum* and that the French had the right to start a war.

Bellum Justum

The Latin phrase *bellum justum* means "just war," and it carried significant importance in the Late Middle Ages. Roman Catholic theology in the Middle Ages did more than tell people if they were sinning or condemn heretics to be burned. The theology and the critical thinking of prominent scholars like Saint Thomas Aquinas set standards and guidelines by which rulers would follow laws and rules of conduct. These precepts would define what was moral or immoral regarding public policy. A just war was defined by three elements: *jus ad bellum* (the right to go to war), *jus in bello* (right conduct in war), and *jus post bellum* (justice after war). *Jus ad bellum* required that specific criteria be met to justify going to war:

- There has to be a reason for going to war that is both morally sound and valid. This could include recapturing territory that was not rightfully seized.
- Only a recognized authority can declare war. The intent of the conflict must be a just and lasting peace and not to satisfy a desire for personal revenge, conquest, or gain.

---

[i] The Scottish History Society. (2024, June 29). *The Wars of Independence.* Retrieved from Scottishhistorysociety.com: https://scottishhistorysociety.com/the-wars-of-independence/

- There has to be a reasonable chance for success. Pointless wars do not meet the standards for the right to go to war.
- The intentions for the war must be good.
- Other ways of resolving the problem should be tried.
- The benefits need to be proportional to any anticipated destruction or harm.[i]

Philip VI decided that he had checked nearly all the boxes. He had the authority to declare war because he was the king of France, and Edward was a vassal. Philip could say that he was only upholding the laws of France and keeping order, especially the feudal order of vassalage, which was accepted practice and had been for centuries. The just cause was that Edward had not fulfilled his feudal obligations. Moreover, Edward supported the opposition to the French Crown. Philip could claim that seizing Aquitaine was his only alternative since Edward had ignored his obligations as a vassal.

Declaring a just war was a very astute move for the king. Philip VI immediately had the moral high ground, and he could say that he was a defender of law and order. He was reinforcing the obligations of feudalism and the obligations that vassals owed. The nobles of France would understand this and believe what Philip was doing was justifiable. The king was maintaining the order of the realm, which would make sense to the common people, who would be more willing to fight for him in the following engagements as a result. Philip would have an easier time mobilizing resources, including taxation, because he was fighting a just war.

Getting the support of the Catholic Church was very important too. The clergy could preach sermons supporting the effort, and they might even be willing to provide financial support. Alliances could be formed with countries that believed that what Philip was doing was reasonable. Neutral countries could stay on the sidelines, preventing Edward III from recruiting support abroad.

Philip now had control of the narrative of the war to come. He could easily portray what he was doing as a righteous fight, which would keep any dissent to a minimum. To sum it up, Philip could get the support he needed thanks to his decision to declare a just war.

---

[i] Internet Encyclopedia of Philosophy. (2024, June 29). *Just War Theory*. Retrieved from Iep.utm.edu: https://iep.utm.edu/justwar/

The relations between England and France at this time can be considered a high-stakes game of chess. Philip had made one move by declaring a just war, so Edward had to respond. His way of doing it was to reassert his claim to the French throne. Edward stated that he had not violated any code of feudalism because he was the legitimate king of France. The hierarchy in which he was subordinate to Philip was nonexistent. This counter-move could persuade monarchs who were enemies of Philip to ally themselves with Edward since they would be backing a legitimate claim to the French throne.

Meanwhile, Edward was facing a dilemma. He could be fighting a two-front war against the Scots to the north and against the French to the south. He needed to assemble an armed force large enough to deal with France and Scotland if necessary. It would not be easy to do. Edward could appeal to honor and glory, but that was not enough for the pragmatic English barons. They had to be able to gain materially. Edward had to use the possibility of material profit to persuade his nobles to raise troops and fight for him.

War is hell, but in the 14th century, it was a profitable business. Nobles could increase their wealth by going out to fight in wars, which would often include looting and pillaging. In addition, conquered territory could be distributed amongst those aristocrats who proved themselves to be particularly loyal. Edward could easily persuade his nobles that the war against France would be an opportunity to make some money.

This sounds very cynical, but it is important to remember that family meant more than national patriotism at that time. English lords could increase their family's holdings and prestige by going off to fight. The battles were going to take place in France, which meant English estates would be protected from the horrors of war, thanks to the English Channel. Rewards from raiding and ransoming captured French aristocrats could be sizable. And if Edward was successful and was able to take the French crown, there was an opportunity to obtain prestigious titles along with large grants of land in the newly conquered kingdom. These were all reasons to fight on Edward's behalf.

There was another opportunity for Edward to exploit. He knew that his father, Edward II, had been murdered by nobles, and there was always a chance that a disgruntled lord might form a plot or start a rebellion. By fighting a war, Edward could have members of the nobility close to him so that he could watch what they were doing. There was always the possibility that a potential troublemaker might get killed in battle or taken prisoner. If either happened, there would be one less bothersome person Edward had to worry about.

The battlelines were being drawn, and both sides faced a significant cost for future fighting. Wars have always been expensive, and large armies require a combination of tax revenue and loans to pay for expenses. A decisive victory would have been helpful for either side to end the war quickly. In the meantime, considerable planning was needed, and there would be smaller engagements to fight.

Chapter 2: The Battles of Sluys and Crécy

Both sides understood the enormity of the conflict that was going to happen. Preparations included diplomatic outreach as both sides sought to gain allies or at least neutralize other countries from joining the war. Edward III scored a major diplomatic coup when he allied with Holy Roman Emperor Louis IV on August 26th, 1337. The alliance between the two became even closer when Louis proclaimed the English king as the vicar of the Holy Roman Empire in 1338. That did more than give Edward considerable prestige; it also made him look less like an upstart and more like a serious contender for the French throne. Louis IV also permitted Edward III to raise troops in the Holy Roman Empire. This privilege increased Edward's military resources in the war's early years. Edward also solidified relations with Flanders. This was more of an economic alliance than a political one. Flanders and England needed each other to maintain successful commerce.[i]

France also worked to build alliances during this time. One of the most significant alliances was with Genoa, Italy. The Genoese had one of the best navies in the medieval world. What is interesting about the relationship is that there was no formalized treaty. Instead, there was a contract between France and Genoa that required France to pay a substantial amount of money for Genoese warships. There was an

---

[i] Lieberich, H. (2024, March 22). *Louis IV*. Retrieved from Britannica.com: https://www.britannica.com/biography/Louis-IV-Holy-Roman-emperor

upfront payment and ongoing compensation during the duration of the contract, and payment schedules were included.

The Fight in the Channel

Control of the English Channel was a significant contest in the early years of the war. For France, control of the Channel was a critical part of the nation's defense. It would not only mean that the French coastline would be protected from raids, but French control of this waterway would also guarantee that England's supply lines would be severely disrupted. It would be difficult to transport any invasion force if France ruled the waves.

England would obviously need control of the Channel for logistics and supplies. There was another, even more important reason to control the Channel. England relied on maritime trade for economic survival. Wool exports to Flanders required safe passage for merchant vessels. Furthermore, the Channel was where wine from Gascony could be imported, and foodstuffs needed in southeast France could be exported.

There was also a matter of prestige. French dominance in the English Channel could showcase the superiority of the French navy and its ability to protect the homeland. If England were able to command the Channel, it would demonstrate new naval powers for the island nation and prove that England could successfully challenge French power.

Raids on England

The French embarked on a strategy of raiding English seaports along the southern coast, hoping to weaken English maritime capabilities and force Edward to spend more time and energy protecting his ports than attacking France. A series of raids took place in 1338 and 1339.

The first assault hit Portsmouth on March 24th, 1338. Admiral Nicholas Behuchet sailed with a fleet of small ships to Portsmouth, which was not well defended and did not have walls. Portsmouth's shipping and supplies were looted, stores and docks were burned down, and citizens of Portsmouth were killed or taken off as slaves. Regrettably, no English ships contested the French advance on Portsmouth.

Southampton was also a target. On October 4th, 1338, a fleet of French and Genoese ships under the command of Admiral Hugh Quiéret attacked. Southampton did not have lookouts posted, so the town was taken by surprise. The French made off with wool and other valuable commodities after they sacked and burned the seaport. The result of this raid was that for the next forty years, Southampton spent a considerable amount of money rebuilding the town walls and strengthening the protecting castle.[i]

The success at Southampton encouraged the French to continue their attacks along the coast. Plymouth was the next target. The French struck on May 20th, 1339. This time, there was resistance from English soldiers, but several ships were taken by surprise in Plymouth Sound and sank.[ii]

Coastal defenses became a priority for the English, and large garrisons were established at major ports. The costs were already starting to mount, and the demands placed Edward in financial trouble. He was forced to borrow significant amounts of money from Jewish and Italian bankers at high rates of interest. The loss of revenue from the ports also became a significant problem. It was not just the French military raids either; piracy was becoming an issue. Something had to be done, or else England would go bankrupt.

<u>Battle of Sluys</u>

Breaking the French grip on the English Channel was not possible if the English only reacted to raids. They had to move from defensive to offensive positions, and Edward III was more than willing to do that. The French had a large fleet anchored at Sluys in what is now the Netherlands. This prevented English forces and supplies from crossing the English Channel to the Continent. Destroying that fleet would be necessary to take control of the Channel. Moreover, Sluys was strategically located to allow for dominance over maritime trade and communication with the Continent. Edward was certainly up to the task.

A large fleet of approximately 150 English ships was assembled. The armada included large and small vessels and was well equipped with the necessary weapons. Edward recruited sailors from coastal towns and from various parts of the Holy Roman Empire. England was able to gather intelligence about the French fleet's position and size. Thus, Edward was able to plan a battle strategy that had a good chance of success.

In January 1340, the English surprised the French galley fleet at Boulogne, a coastal city in northern France. The raid was a great success.

---

[i] Sotonopedia.wikidot.com. (2024, July 7). *French Raid.* Retrieved from Sotonopedia.wikidot.com: http://sotonopedia.wikidot.com/page-browse:french-raid

[ii] Moorhouse, D. (2022, May 20). *French Raid on Plymouth.* Retrieved from Thehundredyearswar.com: https://thehundredyearswar.co.uk/french-raid-on-plymouth/

The English destroyed eighteen French galleys, twenty-four other ships, and large amounts of naval equipment. The losses meant the French were not able to continue waiting on the southern coast. The English got revenge for those earlier raids with attacks on Dieppe, Le Treport, and Mers in the following months.

Philip ordered the French fleet to be rebuilt and requisitioned merchant ships. Normandy supplied most of the two hundred ships that were eventually collected. The fleet included galleys, royal warships, and 167 merchant vessels. Over nineteen thousand sailors manned these ships under the command of Quiéret and Behuchet. This "Great Army of the Sea" gave Philip two options. He could use it to solidify control of the Channel, thereby choking England's maritime economy and forcing England into bankruptcy, or he could use the ships to invade Edward's kingdom.

Although Gascony was important, Edward decided that he wanted to assist his allies in northeastern France, especially the Flemish people. The only way to do this was to gain control of the English Channel so that men and supplies could be transported. Edward originally wanted to sail against Sluys in late spring, but due to delays, including sailors refusing to muster unless they were paid, he had to wait. On June 4th, 1340, the king's counselors decided to have what was available set sail. Six days later, on June 10th, the council received word that the Great Fleet had arrived at Sluys. The attack had to be reconsidered, and orders were set out to gather more forces and ships. Finally, the English fleet was assembled at Orwell on June 20th. The English ships set sail on June 22nd and were near their objective by the following day.

Edward himself was present for the battle on board a ship. He was in greater danger than he could possibly be on land. Fighting on land gave him the opportunity to flee the battlefield. It was different on the water. There was a genuine chance that the ship he was on might sink and that the English king would drown. Despite the danger, Edward was going to prove that he was capable of leading a force, even at the risk of death. He was not the passive person his father, Edward II, had been.

Sluys resembled a land battle. Ships would come up alongside one another, and the opposing crews would tie the ships together and fight hand to hand on the decks. A serious mistake the French made was to chain ships together. This resulted in single French ships being attacked by English vessels, and other French ships could not come to their rescue since they were chained together.

The English gained the upper hand as the day progressed. Their Flemish allies sailed out from nearby ports and attacked the French rear. When night finally fell, the English had captured 166 French merchant ships and sunk or burned 24 enemy vessels. Only a few galleys and seventeen French ships escaped. The French suffered casualties of anywhere between sixteen thousand and twenty thousand men. Many deaths were due to drowning. Both French commanders had been captured, and they were executed in revenge for their earlier raids. Those French who were able to swim ashore were clubbed to death by Flemish civilians. Bodies washed up on the shores for days afterward. It was a total catastrophe for the French.

It was a magnificent victory for the English, but it was of little strategic importance. The English could control the Channel for a while, but Philip rebuilt the French navy and continued the war on the high seas. Nevertheless, Edward could now transport troops to the Continent, and the victory proved that England could win the fights on sea and land.

A miniature of the Battle of Sluys.'

An Interlude

Medieval warfare was not a twelve-month-a-year affair. There were seasons in which no fighting took place, and there were times when truces were declared. Those periods of inactivity gave opposing armies the opportunity to rest and regroup.

Edward followed up his victory at Sluys by besieging Tournai. The siege was inconclusive because a truce was brokered by Philip and Jeanne (Joan) of Valois, who happened to be Edward's mother-in-law and Philip VI's sister. The Truce of Espléchin was signed on September 25th, 1340, and lasted for nine months, during which Edward was not allowed to wage war against France. Edward agreed to the truce in part because the English Parliament was holding up the military funds.

However, the ceasefire did not last long. A dispute over the succession in the Duchy of Brittany, known as the Bretton War of Succession, was the excuse Edward used to restart the war with France. Another temporary truce, the Treaty of Malestroit, was declared in 1343, but it also did not last long.

. Gascony had been seized by Philip in 1337, and the Battle of Auberoche enabled the English to take back portions of Gascony in 1345. Although these gains were significant, the region remained hotly contested, with territory frequently changing hands.

Battle of Crécy

The Hundred Years' War is known for three significant battles, and the Battle of Crécy was the first. This engagement was a battle in which technological advancements overpowered traditional means of fighting and allowed a vastly outnumbered army to win. Crécy can be viewed as an event that dramatically changed the art of war in western Europe.

After the Battle of Sluys, Edward had the means to move troops into France, and he started several raids. In 1346, Edward led a major campaign, a devastating chevauchée, to plunder the countryside and weaken his enemy. Edward marched through Normandy and intended to move his troops to Calais, whose capture would give the English a significant base for future assaults into France.

Philip wanted to stop Edward's advance, so he gathered a solid army to confront his foe. The two enemies eventually faced each other at Crécy-en-Ponthieu. The French army was enormous; it is estimated that anywhere from twenty thousand to forty thousand men were under Philip's command. The French army included knights, men-at-arms, infantry, and Genoese crossbowmen who were serving as mercenaries. The English had approximately sixteen thousand men. They were grossly outnumbered, but the English king had a secret weapon at his disposal.[i]

Edward's Ace

The English longbow was a six-foot yew archery bow that discharged a feathered arrow a cloth yard (about thirty-seven inches). It was essentially the machine gun of the Middle Ages. The comparison with a crossbow, the other archery weapon of choice, was pretty stark. The English longbow could discharge an arrow at the rate of one every five seconds; the crossbow's rate was one bolt every two minutes. Moreover, the crossbow had to be reloaded by using a winch. The crossbow had a range of approximately 200 yards, and the English longbow had a range of nearly 350 yards. The English longbow was fired at a high trajectory and would descend at an angle. The crossbow's trajectory was flat.

Philip had four thousand Genoese crossbowmen, and Edward had seven thousand archers, all of whom played a decisive role in the fighting.

Aerial Slaughter

The Battle of Crécy was waged on August 26th, 1346. Edward III was the overall commander of the English army, and his son, who was also named Edward, was commander of one of the divisions despite being only sixteen years old. Ordinarily, the constable of France would have commanded the French army, but the constable had been taken prisoner earlier. Philip VI was in command of the French army, and his inability to lead was quickly noticeable.

Edward had his army arranged in three divisions and placed his archers on the flanks in a V formation. That was intended to maximize the archers' field of fire. The archers were also positioned behind freshly dug pits with wooden stakes that were rammed into the ground to disrupt any cavalry charge. The English infantry was in the center.

The French were lined up with the Genoese crossbowmen in front and the armored cavalry behind. Philip's strategy was fairly typical. The Genoese would move forward and fire a volley to disrupt the English ranks. The armored cavalry would then roar down the field, crash into

---

[i] BritishBattles.com. (2024, July 7). *Battle of Crecy*. Retrieved from BritishBattles.com: https://www.britishbattles.com/one-hundred-years-war/battle-of-crecy/

the enemy lines, and create chaos. Foot soldiers would mop up, following behind the cavalry.

The battle started at 4 p.m. An unexpected rainstorm broke out as the battle got under way. The English archers removed their bowstrings and covered them so they would not get wet. The Genoese were not able to do that. Consequently, their bowstrings were loose because they were wet. The Genoese discharged a volley, but the bolts fell short of their targets. It was then time for the English to respond.

Jean Froissart was a French historian of the time, and this was his report of the English response: "The English archers each step forth one pace, to the bowstring to his ear, and let their arrows fly; so wholly and so thick that it seemed as snow."[1]

The English volley staggered the Genoese formation, and the mercenaries began to retreat.

Chivalry's Blunder

The Code of Chivalry was taken seriously by the French nobility. Chivalry emphasized bravery and honor. The code also expected French knights to engage in direct combat. Philip saw the Genoese retreating in what appeared to be a cowardly fashion. A seasoned commander would have taken stock of the situation, realized the English archers were deadly, and paused the army's advance. Philip did not do that. Furious at the retreating mercenaries, Philip ordered his cavalry forward and charged them with cutting down the retreating cowards. The French armored cavalry surged forward, killed the crossbowmen who were in the way, and galloped straight into a massacre.

The French attempted multiple charges, but they were cut down by barrages of arrows. Finally, at close to midnight, Philip abandoned the battlefield, and what was left of the French army retreated. The English won a decisive victory.

The butcher's bill for the French was staggering. It is estimated that French casualties were in the neighborhood of thirteen thousand to fourteen thousand men. The losses included important nobles. France lost the duke of Lorraine and the count of Blois. Two important allies, John, the blind king of Bohemia, and the king of Majorca, were among the dead. English losses were somewhere between one hundred and

---

[1] BritishBattles.com. (2024, July 7). *Battle of Crecy*. Retrieved from BritishBattles.com: https://www.britishbattles.com/one-hundred-years-war/battle-of-crecy/

three hundred men.[i]

Edward would follow up on this victory by laying siege to Calais, which fell in 1347. The long-term significance of this battle was momentous. The power of the English longbow decimated chivalric warfare and the codes of conduct on the battlefield. The longbow would continue to be a primary weapon in the English army throughout the Hundred Years' War. What happened at Crécy demonstrated that a rain of arrows could blunt armored cavalry charges. Edward's son was also one of the heroes of the battle. This teenager would become one of the best field commanders of the English army. He would become known as the Black Prince.

Crécy was a significant win for the English, but England and the rest of Europe were about to confront an even fiercer enemy that no arrow could stop or defeat.

---

[i] Hickman, K. (2019, September 3). *Hundred Years' War.* Retrieved from Thought.co: https://www.thoughtco.com/hundred-years-war-battle-of-Crécy-2360728

Chapter 3: The Black Death and the Black Prince

The story goes that the Black Death originated in the Genoese seaport of Kaffa, located in the Crimean Peninsula. Perhaps it started to spread when the Mongols besieged the city and tossed plague-infested corpses over the wall; this has not been corroborated. What we do know is that this pandemic spread along the Silk Road, and Kaffa was a terminal on the trade route. The European origin of the Black Death might have been anywhere in the Black Sea, and it was spread to Europe on ships coming out of that region.[1]

What we do know is that a fleet of ships from the Black Sea docked in Messina, Sicily, in October 1347, and most of the sailors on board were either dead or gravely ill with a disease that residents had never seen before. The port authorities quickly ordered the ships out of the harbor, but the infection had already jumped from the ships onto the docks. Europe was about to experience the worst pandemic it had seen in ages.

A Lethal Sickness

In 2020, the world experienced a pandemic. The major difference between that pandemic and what happened in the 14th century is that modern science and research were able to identify the virus and develop a vaccination to protect people from it. There was no such knowledge in

---

[1] Kiger, P. J. (2023, September 8). *How the Black Death Spread Along the Silk Road.* Retrieved from History.com: https://www.history.com/news/silk-road-black-death

1347. The Black Death spread quickly and killed rapidly. People could show signs of infection one day and be dead within forty-eight hours. Nobody quite understood where it came from. Writers of the day, like Giovanni Boccaccio, an Italian poet, commented on it. "The mere touching of the close appeared to itself to communicate the malady to the toucher."[i]

Boccaccio commented further in his work, *The Decameron*, about how the Black Death hit Florence and the features of the disease. The disease soon began to propagate and spread in all directions. Black spots appeared in many cases on the arm or the thigh, initially few and large before becoming numerous and small. The poet goes on to note that in Florence, more than 100,000 people died and that bodies piled up outside doorways.[ii]

The mortality figures were gruesome, and although some places, such as Milan, did not suffer significantly, Paris reportedly buried one hundred dead each day when the Black Death reached its peak. Estimates vary, but the death toll in Europe between 1347 and 1352 ranged somewhere between twenty-five million and thirty million people. To give an idea of how devastating the Black Death was, the population of Europe would not return to pre-1347 levels until around 1550.[iii]

Impact on England and France

The Black Death swept over Europe, going as far north as the Scandinavian countries. England and France were not immune. Both nations suffered as the war was going on.

The plague tore apart the societies of both countries. Paris experienced a death toll of close to 50 percent of its population, and seaports like Marseilles were hit hard. London experienced a similar death toll. The economic impact was severe.

France and England were hit with labor shortages brought on by the Black Death. Agricultural output dropped, as peasants either died or fled the area for their lives. Normandy was already dealing with damage

---

[i] Editors, H. (2023, March 28). *Black Death*. Retrieved from History.com: https://www.history.com/topics/middle-ages/black-death

[ii] Kiger, P. J. (2023, September 8). *How the Black Death Spread Along the Silk Road*. Retrieved from History.com: https://www.history.com/news/silk-road-black-death

[iii] Cartwright, M. (2023, April 5). *Black Death*. Retrieved from Worldhistory.org: https://www.worldhistory.org/Black_Death/

caused by the war, and now it had to face the pandemic. It experienced a steep drop in crop harvests. A subsequent rise in food prices happened in both countries. A combination of a drop in tax revenues and the death of military-aged men caused both sides to cut back on military operations.

However, the stalemate caused by the Black Death did not mean the war was over. The two sides would continue to fight.

The Black Prince

Prince Edward earned his spurs at Crécy, much to the delight of his proud father. The prince would soon be leading military campaigns into France, gaining glory for himself and ruin for any peasant who stood in his way. Warfare in the 14th century was dominated by the Code of Chivalry, which dictated what was expected of a knight.

Troubadours and poets wrote verses about chivalry and the acts of virtuous knights who embraced the rules. Jean Froissart, the primary French historian of the day, waxed poetic over the behavior of Prince Edward and other knights considered worthy of renown for their chivalrous behavior. Chivalry would be a goal for military men long after the Hundred Years' War. The works of Sir Walter Scott and other authors of the Romantic period of the 19th century embellished the noble definition of it. It makes sense that authors of fiction and poets would write so much about chivalry and glorify it. When looking at what was written in comparison to what happened, it is pretty clear that the story of chivalry contained more fantasy than fact.

The Clash of Image Versus Reality

Chivalry conceived an idea of the perfect knight. He was a man who was generous and noble in spirit, courageous in battle, and kind and fair to noncombatants and prisoners of war. Combat was supposed to be noble and honorable, with explicit shows of mercy.

This was the stuff of ballads, but it was not the reality of war. Knights were professional killers, and they were not above murdering people or performing underhanded acts such as ambushes. Combat was rarely honorable, and one of the best examples is the Battle of Crécy. French knights charged across the battlefield and were cut down by English longbowmen. The French did not abandon the cavalry charge tactic and repeatedly attacked the English, suffering horrible casualties as a result. The honor of single combat, of fighting face to face, was replaced by archery volleys.

A knight's reputation was not based on the mercy he showed but on the number of enemies he killed. It was the accomplishments on the battlefield that made a knight famous. These armored warriors had an unfair advantage most of the time. They rode on powerful horses and wore suits of armor that could weigh as much as sixty pounds. A common foot soldier had no chance against somebody bearing down on them like a Sherman tank. A disadvantage was that the metal could heat up on a hot summer day, causing dehydration, and English archers made the French knights more vulnerable. Nevertheless, the chances of a fully armored knight surviving the battle were pretty good.[i]

Treatment of Civilians

Chivalry expected knights to protect the innocent and not harm women and children. However, that was not always the case. Knights were part of the nobility, and they considered peasants inferior and expendable. Medieval warfare glorified violence, and knights destroyed villages and ravaged crops as a routine part of their job.

An example of knights going rogue was the sack of Limoges. Prince Edward besieged this French city in September 1370. Froissart mentioned in his writings that the Black Prince had a violent passion and permitted his men to run amok. The French historian's account of what happened might have been a little exaggerated, as the claim that thousands of people were killed is not substantiated. What was true is that the indiscriminate killing of noncombatants took place, and the city was looted and burned.

---

[i] Medieval Chronicles.com. (2024, July 10). *"The Dark Side of Chivalry: Exploring the Brutal Realities of Medieval Combat."* Retrieved from Medievalchronicles.com: https://www.medievalchronicles.com/medieval-life/code-of-chivalry/the-dark-side-of-chivalry-exploring-the-brutal-realities-of-medieval-combat/

The siege of Limoges.*

The one thing that destroyed the image of honorable chivalry in the Hundred Years' War was the chevauchée. This was a military strategy that involved a rapidly moving large-scale raid. The essential purpose of the chevauchée was to devastate the countryside. The raiders would burn crops, pillage, and destroy villages, essentially crippling the enemy's economy. The raid would erode the financial support raised from taxes and disrupt food supplies. This strategy was considered a great success if it caused a famine in the area.

It was a medieval form of psychological warfare. The raiders intended to undermine the local population and create instability and an overall atmosphere of terror. The raiders would deliberately bypass fortified positions in their attacks. They lived off the land and did not have to have supply trains to slow them down. The military objective of the chevauchée was to provoke the enemy into fighting. By creating chaos, enemy troops would be drawn out from fortified positions and into the open country, where they might be at a disadvantage.[i]

These raids were a blatant disregard of any of the tenets of chivalry. It was an opportunity to attack defenseless people, rob them of their property, and destroy whatever the raiders could not carry away. There was no honor involved, but it did not matter. War is hell, and the knights were going to prove that was true.

Honor Among Rogues

An example used to show the Black Prince was noble and chivalrous was his treatment of King John (r. 1350-1364) after the French monarch was captured. Chivalry was a set of rules that governed the conduct of nobles toward each other. Anyone of lower rank could be treated poorly.[ii]

There was a practical reason to be polite to noble prisoners of war. A ransom culture had developed by this time. Capturing a noble opponent was comparable to winning the lottery. A baron could fetch a very high price, so it was worth treating those prisoners well so that they survived and could be bought back by their families. King John, for example, commanded a very high price for his ransom. On the other side of the equation, it was possible that the tables would be turned later and that the captor could become a prisoner. It made sense, therefore, to always treat one's prisoners well because they might be one's jailers later.[iii]

Chivalry was always a nice code of ethics, but it was not rigorously enforced. Knights on the battlefield and in enemy territory behaved like a ravaging pack of wolves most of the time. Much of the tragedy of the Hundred Years' War resulted from these warriors ignoring any rules of civility. Prince Edward was known as the Black Prince, which was an appropriate moniker for the man. He had a very sinister side.

---

[i] History Skills.com. (2024, July 10). *Chevauchée: The Brutal War Tactics Knights Used to Terrorize the People of Medieval Europe.* Retrieved from Historyskills.com: https://www.historyskills.com/classroom/year-8/chevauchée/

[ii] Gershon, L. (2023, August 18). *Chivalry Was Established to Keep Thuggish Medieval Knights in Check.* Retrieved from History.com: https://www.history.com/news/chivalry-knights-middle-ages

[iii] Couhlan, S. (2013, January 24). *Medieval Warfare Had Well-Organized 'Ransom Market.'* Retrieved from BBC.com: https://www.bbc.com/news/education-21168437

The Chevauchée of the Black Prince

The stress of the Black Death and the enormous expenses brought on by war strained the resources of France and England. Both countries needed a break from hostilities, and the Truce of Calais, which was expected to last for four years, was signed in 1347 between the two warring nations. It would give both countries a well-needed rest. King Edward III turned his attention to diplomacy, strengthened alliances with the Low Countries, and supported John of Montfort in the Breton War of Succession.

Hostilities resumed in 1350 with the naval Battle of Winchelsea, which was not a victory for the English. Edward instituted some reforms to fund the war, including new taxes and more efficient means of collecting the money that was due. Victories at Saintes in 1351 and Mauron in 1352 strengthened the English position in Gascony and aided the English-supported faction in the War of the Breton Succession.

By this time, Philip VI had died (he passed away in 1350), and his successor was his son, John II. The king's personal representative in southern France was John, Count of Armagnac. The count was a proponent of taking the offensive against the English, and he conducted raids into Gascony, devastating the farming areas. Edward decided that there had to be a forceful response. A grand chevauchée was planned against French holdings in southern France. The Black Prince was given command of the Gascon troops and arrived in Bordeaux on September 20th, 1355. Armagnac was going to be the primary target, and Prince Edward began his campaign of destruction with approximately six thousand men on October 5th.

What happened next was a campaign of senseless damage. The English torched Armagnac, destroying fields of grain and sacking towns. John of Armagnac had a larger army, but he deliberately avoided battle with the Black Prince. The English were free to burn and pillage everything in their path. The raid extended for approximately three hundred miles to the city of Narbonne. French chroniclers might have exaggerated the extent of the destruction, but it is safe to say that southern France suffered extensive economic ruin. The campaign finally ended on December 2nd, 1355.

Prince Edward as a Knight of the Garter.[i]

Battle of Poitiers

The English decided to follow up the success of Gascony with another large-scale raid. Accordingly, the Black Prince set out from Gascony with a substantial force and headed toward the Loire Valley, one of the principal agricultural areas of France. Once again, the English pillaged their way through the countryside and plundered undefended towns. King John II of France knew that he had to respond to the assault on his country, so he gathered a substantial force. His immediate objective was to intercept the Black Prince, block the English retreat toward Gascony, and force them to fight. He was assisted in this by reconnaissance units that carefully followed the movements of the English army.[i]

---

[i] History Skills.com. (2024, July 10). *The Dramatic Battle of Poitiers: Where the Black Prince Captured the King of France*. Retrieved from Historyskills.com:
https://www.historyskills.com/classroom/year-8/battle-of-poitiers/

Prince Edward was followed in earnest by King John, and the two armies finally faced each other on September 19th, 1356, a few miles outside the city of Poitiers. The French had an army of approximately sixteen thousand men facing an English force of around six thousand soldiers.

The French were painfully aware of Crécy's lessons and tried to respond in a way that would offset the English longbowmen. John divided his army into four parts. The front rank had three hundred knights accompanied by German mercenary pikemen. This group would attack the archers and eliminate the threat. Three other groups of infantry and dismounted cavalry would follow behind.

The Black Prince demonstrated his military genius in this battle. He ordered his left wing to stage a fake retreat, which provoked the French knights into charging what they thought were retreating English soldiers. The archers turned around and fired volleys of arrows at the French. Although French armor was able to deflect the arrows, English archers simply adjusted their targets and shot the horses instead.

The second group of French moved forward, but they withdrew to regroup after a while. The third group thought these soldiers were retreating, so they turned back, causing considerable confusion.[i]

Finally, the fourth group, under the personal command of King John, advanced. The Black Prince ordered his entire army to attack. He had a reserve cavalry force that was sent around the French flank and attacked the enemy from the rear. That maneuver caused considerable panic within the French ranks, and the army collapsed. King John was captured. The battle was over.

The English lost approximately one thousand men, and the French lost close to four thousand. More importantly, many important French nobles lay dead on the battlefield, and the king was a prisoner of England. Once again, the English and their longbowmen had scored an impressive victory.[ii]

France was descending into administrative confusion, with its king a prisoner of its enemy.

---

[i] New World Encyclopedia. (2024, July 10). *Battle of Poitiers*. Retrieved from New World Encyclopedia.org: https://www.newworldencyclopedia.org/entry/Battle_of_Poitiers

[ii] Adams, S. (2024, July 10). *Battle of Poitiers*. Retrieved from Britannica.com: https://www.britannica.com/event/Battle-of-Poitiers-French-history-1356

Chapter 4: The Art of War

The Hundred Years' War was much more than battles and military campaigns. It was a time of intense change in the art of warfare and military strategy. Land battles shifted away from overreliance on cavalry charges, and siege warfare became more sophisticated. Technology made battlefields a place of immense slaughter, and refined notions of chivalry gave way to pragmatic assessments of risk.

This chapter will be devoted to the way military matters evolved during this conflict.

<u>Adaptability Was Essential</u>

The English longbow was the weapon of disaster on the battlefields of the Hundred Years' War. The casualty figures from the three major battles substantiate that claim. The longbow was not the product of a medieval Manhattan project, though. In fact, this weapon had been around for quite a while.

It originated in Wales. Years earlier, Welsh archers used the longbow against English invaders and killed a substantial number with it. King Edward III recognized the value of archery and permitted the sport to be practiced on Sundays. Welch archers became part of the English military, and they brought their bows with them.

The armored cavalry charge had been a staple of European warfare for centuries, and the French were very comfortable with it. One irony is that no French visitor to England apparently noticed the English longbow, and if they did, it was not reported back to the French government. It was an oversight that would result in thousands of casualties in the war.

The English knew the value of their archers. Edward III and the Black Prince had large numbers of archers in their armies. Of course, there was a risk of using new technology on the battlefield. If English bowmen at Crécy had not kept their bowstrings dry, it is possible their volleys would have fallen short. The French would have trampled them as a result.

The English longbow had some drawbacks, though. It required extensive training to master, and the draw force on the bow was 160 to 180 lbf (pound-force). The archers were vulnerable at close range because they did not have the same armor as the infantry. They needed protection in front of them and ordinarily formed on the flanks of the army instead of the center.

A significant problem arose in the 1350s. Yew wood was the primary material used to make the longbow. England began to suffer from a shortage of that tree. Ultimately, ships were required to pay a fee of four staves per ton of goods imported into English ports. The longbow remained a potent weapon until it was replaced by firearms.[i]

Cannons and Gunpowder

The first reference made to cannons by the English was in the siege of Berwick in 1333. Edward III used cannons at the Battle of Crécy and would later employ them to bombard Calais.

Gunpowder is essential for the use of artillery. A form of gunpowder was used in China centuries before, but it was used mainly in ceremonies and to launch fireworks. Europe advanced the science of metal casting so that large church bells could be produced. It was a relatively small step from casting bells to mass producing metal tubes that launched hell. The cannon would evolve throughout the Hundred Years' War.

The cannon was very primitive in its early stages, but it was refined over time. Carved stone balls were the original ammunition and would ultimately be replaced by cast metal cannonballs. The gun castings eventually permitted a more powerful charge of gunpowder to be used without the cannon exploding.

One challenge that was present in the early stages was the extremely heavy weight of the cannon. They could not be used in the lightning raids the English employed against the French in the mid-14th century.

---

[i] Hickman, K. (2020, March 2). *Hundred Years' War: English Longbow*. Retrieved from Thoughtco.com: https://www.thoughtco.com/hundred-years-war-english-longbow-2361244

However, the psychological effect of a cannon's noise and belching smoke would unnerve any opponent. The best use for these military monsters was in sieges.[i]

Battle Tactics

Momentous changes were made in the way battles were conducted during the Hundred Years' War. The reliance on armored cavalry faded, and other strategies began to be employed for maximum gain.

The chevauchées were little more than murder raids, but they did serve the purpose of trying to force the enemy to respond in a pitched battle. After the losses at Crécy and Poitiers, the French avoided formal battles, which was not very popular with the French aristocracy but did counteract the intention of the chevauchée. Those raids were not only devastating; they were also expensive. It was not long before they became exercises in diminishing returns, as pillaged areas could offer nothing for future raiders. A Fabian strategy of withdrawing and holding back from large-scale combat became effective for the French since it made the English waste their money.

Longbows were effective on the battlefield but not in siege warfare. The latter half of the Hundred Years' War was dominated by sieges as the English sought to conquer land rather than exploit it for plunder. The French developed better cannons, and they were able to successfully end major sieges such as that of Orléans.

Professional Armies

The traditional means of raising troops was to have levies drawn up. Soldiers would come from the lands and estates owned by loyal aristocrats and serve for a given period, which might have been only a month. The only professional standing contingents of soldiers were the companies that protected the king. This changed radically in the 14th century.

Mercenaries, soldiers for hire, were being used more often. The practice of hiring foreigners for defense became popular in Italy. Italian city-states had the money to pay for mercenaries, and large professional armies of soldiers for hire became the norm. One of the most notorious mercenary companies was the White Company, which was commanded by Englishman John Hawkwood. The law of primogeniture provided for

---

[i] Knighton, A. (2016, June 27). *How Artillery Evolved in the 100 Years' War*. Retrieved from Warhistoryonline.com: https://www.warhistoryonline.com/medieval/artillery-100-years-war.html

the supply of professionally trained men. The eldest son of a nobleman would inherit all of his father's estate according to the rules of primogeniture. Younger sons were out of luck and had to find a way to make a living. Military training was part of their upbringing, so serving as a mercenary permitted these men to do well financially.

Mercenaries posed a severe problem because they owed no allegiance to anybody but their employer. Domestic laws did not mean much to them, and the mercenaries were prone to raiding and robbery. They became a serious social problem that Niccolo Machiavelli would later condemn in his seminal work, *The Prince*. Mercenaries had a tendency to change sides if the price was right. Hugh Calverley is one example. He initially fought for the French under Bertrand du Guesclin during the Hundred Years' War. Later, he switched sides and served under the Black Prince.

War was what a mercenary lived for, as times of peace meant unemployment. An interesting story about the attitude of mercenary soldiers involved John Hawkwood. He was going somewhere and was greeted by a priest on the way with the friendly salutation "Pax Vobiscum" ("Peace be with you"). The English mercenary cursed the startled prelate for wishing to deprive Hawkwood of his livelihood. This story is apocryphal, but it is interesting nonetheless.[i]

England and France transitioned during the Hundred Years' War into having professional armies. An obvious reason was that mercenaries could not be trusted to stay loyal. Troops needed to be able to fight for extended periods of time, and local militias could not be asked to spend a year or more traveling from battlefield to battlefield. A growing sense of nationalism also helped. Men could be recruited to protect their country and their families. Mercenaries continued to be a source of soldiers in Italy, but elsewhere, they were gradually replaced by standing armies.

Siege Warfare

The walls surrounding Constantinople were thought to be impenetrable. They were enormous and successfully withstood attempts to take the city for centuries.

---

[i] Knighton, A. (2016, September 6). *A Force to Be Reckoned With: Mercenaries in the Hundred Years' War*. Retrieved from Warhistoryonline.com:
https://www.warhistoryonline.com/medieval/mercenaries-hundred-years-war.html

The English were very familiar with building fortified places. King Edward I created a string of castles in Wales to discourage any local insurrections. These enormous structures made any attacker give up hope of taking them. Sieges would become more predominant as the Hundred Years' War progressed.[i]

A common siege strategy was to surround a castle or city and cut off all supplies and reinforcements. The intent was to starve the defenders into submission. The blockade could last for months and reduce the civilians trapped inside to eating rats and chewing on grass to survive.

A direct assault was an alternative, but it would almost always result in heavy casualties. Digging tunnels underneath the walls or towers and filling the space with combustible materials was a commonly used tactic. This could cause part of the wall to collapse, but it required skilled miners to be successful.

Psychological warfare was used as well. Displaying the heads of captured soldiers or torturing prisoners of war in view of the walls were means of getting inside the heads of the defenders and demoralizing them. Soldiers could be sneaked into a fortified area to spread rumors or create a fifth column (a group that undermines a larger group or nation from within) to create panic and fear.

Siege towers were standard medieval equipment, and trebuchets slung stones and incendiary devices against the walls and into the enclosed area. The most successful weapon used in sieges was cannons. The old curtain walls of fortified places were little match for artillery, which improved significantly as the war went on.

Prolonging a siege had severe consequences. Defenders were routinely offered the opportunity to surrender before the siege began. The terms would include safe conduct for the defenders and civilians or lenient treatment once the city or castle surrendered. Refusing to surrender resulted in very harsh consequences. If the walls were breached, the garrison would be massacred at the very least. A city could be looted and burned while civilians were killed and raped. This was meant to serve as a warning to other cities. King Henry V of England besieged Rouen for six months and caused a severe famine. The town

---

[i] Medievalchronicles.com. (2024, July 10). *A Brutal and Transformative Conflict: Exploring the Battles & Sieges of the Hundred Years' War*. Retrieved from Medievalchronicles.com: https://www.medievalchronicles.com/medieval-battles-wars/a-brutal-and-transformative-conflict-exploring-the-battles-sieges-of-the-hundred-years-war/

ultimately surrendered on January 19th, 1419, but that was after twelve thousand of its citizens were forced out of the city to save food. They had to live in a defensive ditch in front of the city walls.

In his play *Henry V*, William Shakespeare has Henry V give a speech to the governors of Harfleur, demanding the city's surrender. It is a gruesome piece of prose, but it provides us with a clear understanding of what happened to any city that did not accept the terms of surrender. Henry warns the governors that even though he is the king of England, he will not be able to restrain his soldiers. They will rape and pillage to their heart's content. The governors agree to capitulate for the sake of the citizenry.[i]

Cannons were the most effective way of ending sieges quickly. Mighty walls that had withstood traditional siege tactics crumbled before cannon barrages.

The period of the Hundred Years' War holds an interesting historical irony. Just as the war finally ended in 1453, the walls of Constantinople, fortifications that had withstood large-scale assaults for one thousand years, were being blasted to powder by the monstrous cannons of the Ottomans.

Naval Warfare

The discussion of the Hundred Years' War often gets bogged down in explaining the various land battles. This means that combat on the high seas is usually ignored, which is unfortunate, as naval warfare changed during this time.

The fighting on the water was all about control of the trade routes. As mentioned earlier, mastery of the English Channel was essential. French and English ships battled for supremacy, and dominance of the water would often change hands. Maritime strategies, ship designs, and battle tactics evolved during the Hundred Years' War.

Both sides used blockades early in the war. The intention was to restrict the movement of troops, trade goods, and supplies. This gradually went from being a military exercise to economic warfare. The English used their ships to protect merchant vessels and disrupt French shipping. On the other hand, the French made use of raids along the English southern seacoast to prevent the importation of Gascon wine

---

[i] Shakespeare, W. (2024, July 10). *Henry V-3.3.1*. Retrieved from Folger.edu: https://www.folger.edu/search/?q=Harfleur&area=works&work=henry-v

and other goods from southern France.

Naval warfare heavily influenced diplomacy. The French entered into agreements to acquire additional ships with Genoa, Castile, and Denmark. Both the English and the French intervened in the Castilian succession in the 1360s, primarily to gain access to the Castilian fleet.

Ports became essential parts of military strategy. Calais was besieged because of its importance as a cross-channel port. The Breton ports were also coveted.[i]

Mercenaries were used on land, but the ocean had privateers and pirates. The port of Fowey in Cornwall was a nest of English privateers. Fowey received licenses from the English Crown to attack French vessels. Known as the Gallants of Fowey, these privateers operated out of the port, and several became infamous. Mark Mixtow operated a group of three ships, and a Dutch pirate named Hankyn Seelander had a privateer's license granted to him in 1442. A significant problem occurred once the war was finally over because the pirates did not stop their attacks on shipping.

Ships and War Vessels

Shipbuilding and the maintenance of ships were expensive, so the war fleets were raised by impressing merchant vessels. The Cinque Ports in southeastern England were required to provide the crown with ships and sailors. This was to the economic disadvantage of the merchants and shipowners because they would be deprived of their ships during the height of the fishing and trading seasons. Moreover, they were not given payment for the vessels. If a ship was sunk, captured, or damaged, there was no compensation for the loss.[ii]

The English needed ships that had a considerable carrying capacity. The cogs were the merchant vessels of choice for impressment. The cog had a rounded, deep hull with a single large sail and a high freeboard (the distance from the waterline to the upper deck). They could carry large numbers of men, and their heavy build gave them an advantage in close-quarter combat.

---

[i] MSW. (2009, February 9). *Naval Warfare in the 100 Years' War*. Retrieved from Weaponsandwarfare.com: https://weaponsandwarfare.com/2009/02/10/naval-warfare-in-the-100-years-war/#google_vignette

[ii] MSW. (2009, February 9). *Naval Warfare in the 100 Years' War*. Retrieved from Weaponsandwarfare.com: https://weaponsandwarfare.com/2009/02/10/naval-warfare-in-the-100-years-war/#google_vignette

Impressing merchant vessels was not very popular, and King Henry V finally realized that a permanent fleet was necessary. Through capture, purchase, and construction, a royal fleet of approximately thirty-five vessels was created in the 1420s.

The French had other needs. They wanted ships that were smaller and faster for raids. The galley was their preferred vessel. The French had a shipyard in Rouen, the Clos de Galées, whose sole purpose was to build galleys.[i]

Another vessel used during the Hundred Years' War was the caravel. These smaller ships were very agile. What made them stand out was that they were also used to carry cannons. They were sturdier than the typical merchant ship.

Several important naval battles were fought during the Hundred Years' War. We have already mentioned the Battle of Sluys. During that battle, the English used longbowmen to decimate the French crews. Apparently, the French did not take notice of the use of those archers since they did not warn the French Crown of the danger. The French would pay dearly for that six years later at Crécy. An important battle that was fought just before Sluys was Arnemuiden. This was the first naval battle that used artillery.

A pivotal battle on the high seas was fought at La Rochelle from June 22nd to June 23rd, 1372. The fleet that opposed the English that day was not French. France had an alliance with Castile, and a Castilian fleet sailed out to do battle with the English. The Castilian fleet was commanded by a Genoese admiral, Ambrosio Boccanegra. The Castilians won a complete victory over the English, and the defeat undermined England's strategic plans for the defense of Gascony.[ii]

The conduct of the Hundred Years' War started to change in the 1360s. King John of France was an English prisoner, which affected military strategy and diplomatic relations. It would seem that the French were devastated, the English were in full control of the situation, and the hostilities would soon permanently cease. However, in a few years, everything would be turned upside down.

---

[i] MSW. (2009, February 9). *Naval Warfare in the 100 Years' War*. Retrieved from Weaponsandwarfare.com: https://weaponsandwarfare.com/2009/02/10/naval-warfare-in-the-100-years-war/#google_vignette

[ii] Britishbattles.com. (2024, July 10). *Battle of La Rochelle*. Retrieved from Britishbattles.com: https://www.britishbattles.com/one-hundred-years-war/battle-of-la-rochelle/

Chapter 5: Society in Chaos

Daily life was very routine in the Middle Ages. There were famines, natural disasters, and wars, but for most people, the day's main events were the sunrise and sunset. Everything else followed a predictable pattern every day. The Roman Catholic Church and the feudal system were reliable pillars of society. They provided structure and order to society.

Things suddenly changed in the 14th century. Calamity hit western Europe like a hurricane. War and disease were destructive forces, and other problems caused dramatic change. Life became increasingly unpredictable, as natural and political upheavals turned the world on its ear. Things were going to be different moving forward.

<u>Havoc in the Church</u>

The Roman Catholic Church, by and large, entered the 14th century with a degree of optimism. Major heretical groups like the Albigensians had been put down, and the new priestly orders, the Franciscans and Dominicans, were providing better social care to the population and engaging in greater intellectual discourse. However, a significant problem developed in the early days of the century that needed to be addressed.

Rome was a lawless town. Factionalism created disputes between prominent families, and corruption was rampant. Rome was a violent city, and no one was safe, not even the pope. The safety of the pope was a primary concern. In addition, there was pressure from the French king, Philip IV, to relocate out of Rome. The College of Cardinals elected Bertrand de Got of Bordeaux as pope in 1305, and he took the papal name of Clement V. Interestingly, the new pope was politically a subject of England, but he was culturally French.[i]

Given Rome's dangerous situation, Clement decided the best course of action would be to move closer to the French king since he could offer protection. Avignon was a papal territory in France, and Clement moved to the papal court in that city. It was initially meant to be a temporary home for the pope, but it turned out to be a residence for seventy years.

It is inaccurate to say that the Avignon residency was a waste of time. Pope John XXII was a capable administrator who expanded the papal bureaucracy, and Pope Benedict XII worked to institute reforms in the church. The optics, however, were horrible. It gave the perception that the papacy was no longer an independent force for good in society. The fact that all of the popes during the residency were French and that most of the cardinals were French gave the impression that the pope was no more than a puppet of the French king. People began to wonder just how spiritual the higher clergy were.[ii]

The Avignon Papacy promoted the arts, and the papal court was a site of scholarly and artistic activity. The Palais des Papes, the papal residence, was an exemplary symbol of cultural patronage. However, this created the perception that the church was more interested in luxury and fine living.

Reaction to the Plague

This stay in France has been referred to as the "Babylonian Captivity" of the popes. The Black Death broke out in the middle of the pope's residency in southern France. The pope at that time was Clement VI. Like so many theologians, Clement initially attributed the pandemic to divine wrath. This did not mean that the pope descended into superstition. He took proactive measures to try to deal with the devastation. A peculiar one was to consecrate the Rhone River as a cemetery. Contemporary readers may think that's strange, but by consecrating the river, the pope assured that the bodies of thousands of

---

[i] Encyclopedia.com. (2024, July 14). *Avignon Papacy*. Retrieved from Encyclopedia.com: https://www.encyclopedia.com/religion/encyclopedias-almanacs-transcripts-and-maps/avignon-papacy

[ii] HistoryTools.org. (2024, May 25). *The Avignon Papacy: Popes, Politics, and Power in 14th Century Europe*. Retrieved from HistoryTools.com: https://www.historytools.org/stories/the-avignon-papacy-popes-politics-and-power-in-14th-century-europe#google_vignette

dead could be buried in a consecrated space.

Jews were accused of being the cause of the plague, and Clement reacted strongly to this. He issued papal bulls in 1348 that condemned violence against the Jews and announced that anyone blaming the Jews for the disaster was under the influence of the devil. In an act of astounding compassion, Clement VI granted the remission of sins to everyone who died from the plague.[i]

Stories suggesting that the Catholic Church was indifferent to victims of the plague are not accurate. Excavations at Thornton Abbey in England prove that plague victims received care at the monastery, and the church was at the forefront of dealing with the pandemic.[ii] The problem was that society was overwhelmed by the plague. The church did what it could to respond, but there were high mortality rates among the clergy. This led to rapid ordinations of men who had little training, which diminished the quality of pastoral care and spiritual leadership.

The stay in Avignon finally ended in 1377 when the papal court returned to Rome. Unfortunately, this did not mean the end of the trials for this pillar of society. Things got much worse in the following years.

The Western Schism

The papacy's return to Rome in 1377 should have been an occasion for joy and celebration. However, in 1378, Gregory XI, the pope who returned the papacy to Rome, died. His death caused the Romans to riot, and they demanded the election of a Roman for pope or an Italian at the very least. The College of Cardinals elected Urban VI, Archbishop of Bari, as Gregory's successor. Urban had a reputation for being a competent administrator, but he had an abrasive personality. He made some bitter enemies among the College of Cardinals. Those opposed to Urban left Rome and headed to Anagni, which was southeast of Rome, for their own conclave. They claimed that Urban's selection was only meant to please the mob, and they elected Robert of Geneva as pope on

---

[i] Valjak, D. (2017, March 3). *Pope Clement VI: The Generous and Progressive Pope Who Granted Remission of Sins to All People Who Died of the Plague.* Retrieved from Thevintagenews.com: https://www.thevintagenews.com/2017/03/03/pope-clement-vi-the-generous-and-progressive-pope-who-granted-remission-of-sins-to-all-people-who-died-of-the-plague/

[ii] Whelan, E. (2020, February 18). *English Medieval Hospital Shows Horrors of Black Death.* Retrieved from Ancient-origins.net: https://www.ancient-origins.net/news-history-archaeology/black-death-0013302

September 20th, 1378. He took the papal name of Clement VII. Instead of going back to Rome, the newly elected pope went back to Avignon.[i]

Choosing Sides

The Catholic Church had dealt with antipopes in the past. These rivals to the legitimate pope ordinarily faded away. However, this time, the situation was much different. There was one pope at Avignon and another in Rome, and each claimed to be the legitimate head of the Roman Catholic Church. European nations took sides in the matter.

The countries that supported the Avignon Papacy were:

- France
- Scotland
- Castile
- Aragon
- Leon
- Cyprus
- Burgundy
- Savoy
- Naples
- Scotland

Those nations in Europe that backed the pope in Rome were:

- The Holy Roman Empire
- England
- Hungary
- Poland
- Flanders
- Denmark
- Ireland
- Norway
- Portugal
- Poland
- Sweden
- The Republic of Venice[ii]

Religion had nothing to do with the loyalty of any of these countries; national interest governed which side a European nation was on. The two popes had separate agendas and theological differences. Urban VI and Clement VII excommunicated each other and tried to legitimize their claims through alliances with the European nations.

---

[i] Libretexts.org. (2024, July 24). *The Western Schism*. Retrieved from Social.libretexts.org: https://socialsci.libretexts.org/Courses/Lumen_Learning/Book%3A_Western_Civilization_%28Lumen%29/Ch._08_The_Middle_Ages_in_Europe/09.8%3A_The_Western_Schism

[ii] Libretexts.org. (2024, July 24). *The Western Schism*. Retrieved from Social.libretexts.org: https://socialsci.libretexts.org/Courses/Lumen_Learning/Book%3A_Western_Civilization_%28Lumen%29/Ch._08_The_Middle_Ages_in_Europe/09.8%3A_The_Western_Schism

A Crisis of Conscience

The Western Schism was a disaster for European society. Both popes eventually died, but that did not end the divide. Instead, Benedict XIII was elected to succeed Clement VII in Avignon, and three popes successively followed Urban VI: Boniface IX, Innocent VII, and Gregory XII.

People were torn between the two sides when it came to religion. The structure of the church was impacted, and the laity was unsure which pope's directives were to be obeyed. An interesting development of the Great Schism was a rise in national identity. People not only considered themselves to be Christians but also members of various nations, depending on which pope was supported.[i]

The Councils

The division between the two popes undermined the unity and authority of the Roman Catholic Church, and something needed to be done to end the split. The Council of Pisa was convened in 1409 to end the dispute.

Gregory XII was reigning in Rome, and Benedict XIII was reigning in Avignon at the time. The cardinals in attendance took a steadfast approach to the schism. The two popes were declared heretical and schismatic, disqualifying both. Neither pope recognized that decision, nor did they recognize the third pope, Alexander V, whom the council elected. The Council of Pisa failed to end the problem, although it asserted that the councils had authority over physical matters. Its failure prompted a call for another council to end the dispute.

The Council of Constance convened in Constance, Switzerland, lasting from 1414 to 1418. Three popes, Gregory XII, John XXIII, and Benedict XIII, were present. Everyone realized that the existing conditions in the church could not continue if Catholicism were to survive. Gregory agreed to resign, which was a major step. John was deposed, and Benedict, who refused to abdicate, was excommunicated. With all three popes out of the way, the council elected Oddone Colonna as Martin V on November 11th, 1417. The Catholic Church was now unified.

---

[i] Frithowulf, H. (2023, November 9). *Western Schism: The 14th Century Papal Schism*. Retrieved from Malevus.com: https://malevus.com/western-schism/#how-did-the-western-schism-occur

The Reforms of Constance

Martin V understood that he needed to restore the integrity of the papacy's moral authority. His task was to rebuild the church's spiritual and administrative structures and consolidate its position in society. Martin moved quickly and decisively.

A series of reforms was initiated to deal with the current corruption and inefficiencies in the church. The new pope moved cautiously. The Western Schism had created a weakness that invited heresy to enter the Catholic Church. The Council of Constance condemned the teachings of John Wycliffe and executed Jan Hus, both of whom were accused of deceiving the faithful. Martin V was able to steer the church through this turbulent time. He tried to mediate the Hundred Years' War and issued a papal bull condemning slavery. It can be argued that his pontificate prevented the collapse of the Roman Catholic Church in the 14th century.[i]

The church faced unusual circumstances during the Hundred Years' War, and some damage is understandable. Nevertheless, one of the biggest problems that was not really addressed was the degree to which the Roman Catholic Church hierarchy strayed from its brand. The Catholic Church's reputation was not entirely based on theology. Its commitment to the poor and socially deprived meant it provided much-needed services to the public. However, the ostentation of the higher clergy and the obvious corruption in the lower ranks soured people's attitudes toward an institution they had once revered. The attempts at reform were feeble, and they were not fully carried out.

It is a minor miracle that the Roman Catholic Church survived the Babylonian Captivity of the popes, the Black Death, and the Western Schism. The experiences did not seem to faze the church fathers, and the Renaissance popes appeared to act as if nothing was wrong. That was a false assumption because a great deal of mischief harmed the church and wrecked its reputation. A substantial reformation was waiting to be born.

---

[i] PopeHistory.com. (2024, July 14). *Pope Martin V*. Retrieved from PopeHistory.com: https://popehistory.com/popes/pope-martin-v/

Consequences of the Black Death

Conditions in both England and France in the late 14th century were ripe for social upheaval. The consequences of the Black Death, the on-again, off-again fighting, and the problems in the Roman Catholic Church created breaks in society. Medieval Europe was defined by feudalism. This was a fairly stable system despite all its faults. The common people knew what was expected of them, which made life routine.

That all changed, particularly after the Black Death. Pillars of society were trying to maintain the status quo instead of addressing all of the issues. The common people were getting increasingly angry about the situations in both France and England. Events that bordered on social anarchy started to happen.

There was a drastic reduction in the population, and it would be centuries in some cases before some regions returned to their pre-plague figures. The mortality rate caused labor shortages and an opportunity for peasants to make more money. The scarcity of able-bodied workers and the demand for labor gave the workers considerable leverage. However, the nobility resisted granting the workers more rights.

The Statute of Labourers, which was passed by the English Parliament in 1351, is an example of aristocratic pushback. This law created a maximum wage for laborers that was equal to what was paid before the plague. Moreover, able-bodied individuals were required to work. Real wages did not rise. However, this statute was not well enforced. The long-term effect of the labor shortage was that farm wages in England doubled between 1350 and 1450, but the anger that the statute generated fed into peasant unrest and, eventually, civil disturbances.

The war created dire conditions in France. There were already problems with the destruction of farmland and the lawlessness caused by the chevauchées and brigands who took advantage of the war. The government imposed increasingly heavy taxation to fund the war, but it could not protect the peasants adequately. The Jacquerie, the peasant revolt that broke out in France in 1358, was in reaction to the heavy taxation and the king's inability to protect the French peasants. The unrest was not limited to the countryside either.

The war placed considerable stress on society, leading to heightened tensions in the increasingly crowded cities of both England and France.

Heavy taxation and economic disruption stemming from the conflict placed significant burdens on the urban population. Issues of social inequality also emerged. In France, the bourgeoisie and urban working classes resented the dominance and privileges held by elites in municipal government. In England, economic disparities fueled tensions between wealthy merchants and laborers, contributing to social unrest.

The Peasants' Revolt

The greatest social uprising of the Hundred Years' War was the Peasants' Revolt of 1381. It was not isolated to one part of the country; it spread across England and made its way into London. The roots of the uprising were the economic difficulties brought on by the Black Death, among other causes.

The labor shortages of the Black Death empowered people to ask for more, including better wages and improved working conditions. The nobility did not respond properly; they were more concerned with maintaining the status quo. The Statute of Labourers was a repressive response to legitimate demands from the workers. The English government introduced a poll tax in 1377 to fund military campaigns. It was a flat tax, and everyone paid the same amount, regardless of how much money they were making.

Enforcing the poll tax sparked a revolt. In May 1381, peasants in Fobbing, Essex, refused to pay the poll tax, and their dissent spread throughout southeastern England. The revolt leader, Wat Tyler, who was aided by a radical preacher named John Ball, inspired the peasants to turn on the English gentry. Groups of them attacked the manor houses, destroyed property, and killed aristocrats. More than just property was destroyed, however. The peasants also targeted the tax records and the court rolls, ensuring that any evidence of owed taxes or futile obligations was destroyed.

The revolt gathered followers as supporters from Suffolk and Norfolk joined the crowds. The decision was eventually made to march on London itself. The rebels' demands were radical. They wanted lower taxes, an official end of serfdom, and the removal of royal advisors who they believed were a bad influence on the English king, Richard II.

The rebels entered London on June 13th and ransacked Savoy Palace, the residence of John of Gaunt, who was the king's powerful uncle. On the following day, June 14th, the Tower of London was stormed. The rebels executed Simon Sudbury, Archbishop of Canterbury, and Lord

High Treasurer Robert Hales. These men were killed because they were considered the men who had implemented the oppressive policies.

Richard II was only fourteen years old when he agreed to meet the rebels at Mile End on June 14th. He agreed to the demands for the abolition of serfdom, the reduction of taxes, and the right to freely rent land. A second meeting was held at Smithfield on June 15th, and the lord mayor of London killed Wat Tyler. The rebel leader's death caused the insurrection to disintegrate. Richard reneged on all his promises, and a brutal repression of the peasants ensued.

Richard II meeting with the rebels.[5]

The Aftermath

The Peasants' Revolt shocked the feudal system. It showed the vulnerability of the ruling elite and demonstrated that the common people could gather to form a collective resistance against royal and aristocratic prerogatives. The rules of serfdom were gradually relaxed, and servants were allowed more freedom to move. The poll tax was abandoned, and it was not brought back until 1990.[i]

John Wycliffe and Jan Hus

As discussed earlier, the Roman Catholic Church was battered and bruised by events in the latter half of the 14th century. Theologians who were teaching at universities stepped forward and demanded that substantial reforms be instituted to allow the church to return to its position as a spiritual and moral authority. The two primary reform leaders were John Wycliffe and Jan Hus.

John Wycliffe was a professor at the University of Oxford and the author of the first translation of the Bible into English, the Wycliffe Bible. He was very critical of the temporal authority of the pope and believed that the church was less worried about a person's soul than the money in their purses.

The church was selling indulgences as a means of raising money. By purchasing an indulgence for a set sum, a person could reduce the amount of time they or someone else would spend in purgatory. Wycliffe was horrified by this practice and other long-held traditions of the Catholic Church. Wycliffe was fortunate that he had the protection of John of Gaunt. Although he was ultimately banished from Oxford, Wycliffe continued to spread his messages of reform, including questioning the doctrine of transubstantiation. He would ultimately die peacefully in his bed. The same cannot be said for Jan Hus.[ii]

Jan Hus taught at Charles University in Prague and was influenced by Wycliffe's teachings. He lived in Bohemia in the early 14th century, and like Wycliffe, he emphasized scripture over church dogma. He was also a strong opponent of the sale of indulgences and proclaimed that Christ and not the pope was the true head of the church. Jan Hus opposed the church's wealth and insisted that to return to its spiritual mission, the Roman Catholic Church had to divest itself of its worldly power. Finally, Hus believed that scripture needed to be translated into the vernacular so that it was more accessible to ordinary people.

---

[i] BBC.co.uk. (2024, July 14). *The Peasants' Revolt*. Retrieved from BBC.co.uk: https://www.bbc.co.uk/bitesize/topics/z93txbk/articles/zyb77yc#zvrmm39

[ii] Calhoun, D. B. (2012, December 4). *John Wycliffe "The Morning Star of the Reformation."* Retrieved from Cslewisinstitute.org: https://www.cslewisinstitute.org/resources/john-wycliffe-the-morning-star-of-the-reformation/

Suffice it to say that his beliefs got him into serious trouble. His teachings gathered a following, which troubled the church and the temporal rulers of Bohemia. Jan Hus was invited to attend the Council of Constance under the protection of Holy Roman Emperor Sigismund. He arrived in Constance on November 3rd, 1414. Instead of being protected, Hus was arrested and tried for heresy. He was officially condemned on July 6th, 1415. He was offered the chance to recant, but he refused and was burned at the stake.[i]

Both men are considered precursors of the Protestant Reformation, and their writings influenced many of the early Protestant reformers. Hus's death did not return things to normal in central Europe. His followers turned to violence. The Hussite Wars were fought from 1419 to 1434. One consequence of the Hussite Wars was a greater sense of Czech national identity.

When reviewing the social unrest of the late 14th and early 15th centuries, a common theme is the reluctance of the established authority to make necessary changes. The sale of indulgences by the Roman Catholic Church was a terrible idea. The church had extensive estates and could have raised the money it needed by selling some of the land. Such sales would have promoted land ownership by peasants and allowed for the peaceful transition from feudalism to private property ownership. The nobility was not in the mood to share any of its power. If it had done so, the Peasants' Revolt could have ended in an improvement in English society.

The Hundred Years' War continued during these days of social unrest. The war would enter a new phase in 1360 when the Treaty of Brétigny gave England and France a temporary period of peace.

---

[i] Johnhus.org. (2023, February). *Who Was John Hus?* Retrieved from Johnhus.org: https://johnhus.org/content/who-was-jan-hus/

Chapter 6: The Treaty of Brétigny

France and England were exhausted by the end of the 1350s. England had been successful on the battlefield, but it was becoming financially difficult to continue the war effort. France had been economically mangled by the chevauchées and peasant uprisings, which destabilized the north. The heavy ransom demands of the English for the return of King John II added to an already strained financial situation. In addition to these problems, both nations were still trying to recover from the Black Death. It was important for England and France to lay down their weapons and heal. The Treaty of Brétigny was meant to give both sides a rest.

The Demands of Both Sides

England held an ace in its hand at the bargaining table. John II was their prisoner, and if the French wanted to have their king back and restore political sanity to the country, sizable portions of land had to be ceded to the English Crown. Aquitaine, Gascony, Poitou, and several other regions of France were to be given to England. The terms under the transfer were full sovereignty. There would be no homage paid to the French Crown; England was the sole possessor. The French wanted something significant in return for handing over these rich provinces. Edward III was expected to renounce his claim to the French throne. Since the claim to the French throne was a significant reason for the hostilities in the first place, it was hoped that by renouncing the English claim to the crown, the dynastic disputes would come to an end.

The cost of ransoming King John was astronomical. The English received three million gold crowns to return the French king. Its value in modern currency would be approximately $1.5 billion.

The finalized Treaty of Brétigny was signed on October 24th, 1360.

France after the Treaty of Brétigny.*

An event that happened at the time of the treaty's final ratification demonstrates the absurdity of the Code of Chivalry. King John's son, Louis I, Duke of Anjou, was given to the English in a hostage exchange.

Louis escaped, and when King John heard of this, he voluntarily returned to England. It was a gesture that preserved his honor, but it was the last thing that France needed. The French had already paid an enormous sum to get the king back, and now the monarch had returned to captivity. The country needed its king more than John needed his pride.

Years later, a king with dubious morals but greater common sense was taken prisoner by the enemy. Francis I was taken prisoner after the battle of Pavia in 1525. He was forced to sign the Treaty of Madrid in 1526, but he reneged on his word as soon as he was able.[i]

It was hoped that the Treaty of Brétigny would provide a lasting peace, but it did not. Hostilities rose once again in 1369.

Internal Troubles

England was at the pinnacle of its power with the signing of the treaty. This did not mean that the country was immune to internal squabbling and dissent. King Edward III was growing older in years after Brétigny, so this was a period of decline for the king. He lost his beloved wife Philippa in 1369 and became influenced by a mistress named Alice Perrers. Alice took advantage of her influence over the aging king and used it to help her favorites. John of Gaunt and the Black Prince became increasingly more influential at court. The corruption of the government was becoming noticeable, and in 1376, the English Parliament was convened to come up with some reforms.

Known as the Good Parliament, it was in session from April 28th to July 10th, 1376. It replaced some of the corrupt advisors of the king and appointed several new ones who were considered to be competent. Its efforts to reform the administration were short-lived because the next year, John of Gaunt worked to undo all the changes.

---

[i] Vioux, M. (2024, July 19). *Rivalry with Charles V*. Retrieved from Britannica.com: https://www.britannica.com/biography/Francis-I-king-of-France/Rivalry-with-Charles-V

John of Gaunt.[7]

A tragedy of epic proportions hit England in 1376. Edward the Black Prince died on June 8th, 1376. The king would follow his son in death, dying on June 21st, 1377. These two deaths resulted in a ten-year-old boy, Prince Edward's son, to be crowned king as Richard II. England would be forced to deal with the problems that a child monarch presented.

The Plantagenet dynasty is usually seen as the most glorious English dynasty. The Plantagenets ruled over England for more than two hundred years, and men such as Henry I, Richard the Lionheart, and Edward III brought fame and riches to the kingdom. Dark clouds were forming over England in the final days of the 14th century, though. It would take a monarch with charisma and courage to weather the storm. Sadly, the king at the time had neither, and his attitude and poor decisions led to the fall of the House of Plantagenet.

A Boy on the Throne

A child ruler is almost always a source of trouble, and Richard II was no exception. He gained immediate fame when he ended the Peasants' Revolt by making outlandish promises that he ultimately did not keep. While it was an amazing act of courage for the teenager to confront the rebels and persuade them to lay down their arms, it might have instilled in Richard the notion that he was under God's special protection and that, as the king, he could do no wrong.

The country was ruled by Richard's counselors when the king was a minor, but Richard began to assert moral authority as he grew older. He relied on a close group of personal favorites to govern the country. This led to a crisis of authority since Richard became increasingly arrogant and haughty in his decisions.

Things came to the breaking point in 1388 when a group of lords, which became known as the Lords Appellant, took control of the government and prosecuted Richard's advisors. In 1389, Richard appointed new ministers, but he was not inclined to negotiate a compromise with anyone. Richard wanted a stronger monarchy and strict obedience. Initially, he didn't have much opposition from the nobility, who believed that a hierarchical government benefited them. However, nobles were very sensitive to any attempt to curtail their power. They resented the influence Richard's favorites had over the king, which led the Lords Appellant to have them removed. Some of them were executed.[1]

Richard sought revenge against the Lords Appellant. The duke of Gloucester was arrested in 1397 and died under mysterious circumstances. The earl of Arundel was arrested, tried for treason, and

---

[1] Saul, N. (2011, 02 17). *Richard II and the Crisis of Authority*. Retrieved from BBC.co.uK: https://www.bbc.co.uk/history/british/middle_ages/richardii_crisis_01.shtml

beheaded. The earl of Warwick was placed on trial and sentenced to life imprisonment. The archbishop of Canterbury was forced into exile. There were two Lords Appellant left: Thomas Mowbray, Earl of Nottingham, and Henry Bolingbroke.

A Victorian depiction of the Lords Appellant.⁸

Mowbray was closely allied with King Richard II and had been richly rewarded for his steadfast loyalty. His status at court was considerable, though not without controversy. Rumors circulated that Mowbray had played a role in the death of Thomas of Woodstock, Duke of Gloucester—Richard's uncle and a leading figure among the king's critics—who died under suspicious circumstances while in custody. Tensions escalated when Mowbray became embroiled in a bitter dispute with Henry Bolingbroke. Bolingbroke publicly accused Mowbray of treason and of being involved in Gloucester's demise. The conflict was scheduled to be resolved through a trial by combat at Coventry in 1398. However, at the last moment, Richard unexpectedly intervened, halting the duel and instead issuing a double exile—Mowbray was banished for life, while Bolingbroke received a ten-year sentence, which was later reduced. The king's motives remain debated; some interpret the decision as a calculated attempt to neutralize both potential threats to his authority. Isolated and far from the politics of the English court, Mowbray died of plague in Venice the following year.

Henry Bolingbroke

Henry Bolingbroke was the son of John of Gaunt, one of Edward III's sons. Even though he was one of the Lords Appellant, he tried to maintain good relations with Richard. His banishment provided Richard with a tantalizing political opportunity.

Richard II had steadily matured into an autocratic tyrant who wanted to centralize power and succeeded in alienating many powerful barons. Richard tried to bypass Parliament and asserted royal prerogative, which led to tensions between him and the nobility.

His financial policies include heavy taxation and the use of a blank charter. These were documents that were signed by an English subject; the content would later be filled in by the king. It was a medieval version of a blank check.

John of Gaunt died in 1399. Henry Bolingbroke was his successor, and he would become the duke of Lancaster, which was the richest duchy in England. Richard sought the chance to not only weaken a possible opponent but also gain control over the Lancastrian estates. Consequently, the king extended the banishment to a life sentence and seized the Lancastrian properties.

The Final Rebellion

Richard felt secure enough on the throne to launch an expedition to Ireland in May 1399. It was a terrible miscalculation because Henry Bolingbroke was not going to sit quietly in exile. He landed in Yorkshire with a small group of followers in 1399. Henry quickly gained the support of English nobles. They were furious over Richard's confiscation of his lands and realized that any of them could have the same thing happen to them if Richard were still king.

Richard returned to England in July and found that he had no support. He was forced to surrender to Henry Bolingbroke on August 19th. Richard agreed to abdicate if his life was spared.

The king returned to London as a prisoner of Henry on September 1st, 1399. He was immediately imprisoned in the Tower of London. Richard was formally deposed on October 1st, 1399, and on October 13th, Henry Bolingbroke became Henry IV of England.

Richard's Final Days

Richard was allowed to live, but he would be imprisoned and placed under close surveillance. However, a plot was discovered that involved murdering the new king and restoring Richard. This meant the former king's life was now expendable. Unlike Edward II, no blood was spilled when it came to Richard's death. It is believed that he was starved to death at Pontifex Castle around February 14th, 1400.

Richard's stubborn insistence on royal prerogative was the main cause of his troubles. If he had been more open to negotiation and compromise, he might have maintained the loyalty of his nobility. His stubborn refusal to believe that he was wrong and that anyone who opposed him was a traitor caused him to lose his life. He was the last Plantagenet king of England.

The King Is Mad, Part One

France needed time to heal, and everyone hoped that the Treaty of Brétigny would give the country that opportunity. Nobody expected the monarchy to have serious problems, but unfortunately, terrible things happened.

The Treaty of Brétigny was only enforced for a few years. By 1369, new hostilities had erupted. The outcomes were not as one-sided as before, though. The Battle of Pontvallain in 1370 is one example. The French army, under the command of Bertrand du Guesclin, surprised the English forces and wiped them out. It was not a large battle, but it shattered the myth of English invincibility and caused the English to consider shifts in their strategy. It was not going to be as easy to defeat the French as it had been in the past.

The war was entering what is known as the Carolinian Phase. The French were now going on the offensive and were using technological improvements, including body armor for war horses. Fighting was concentrated in southeastern France, and the English were forced to defend their extended borders. The French employed small raids and used Fabian tactics to evade English counterattacks. The English were gradually losing land to the French.

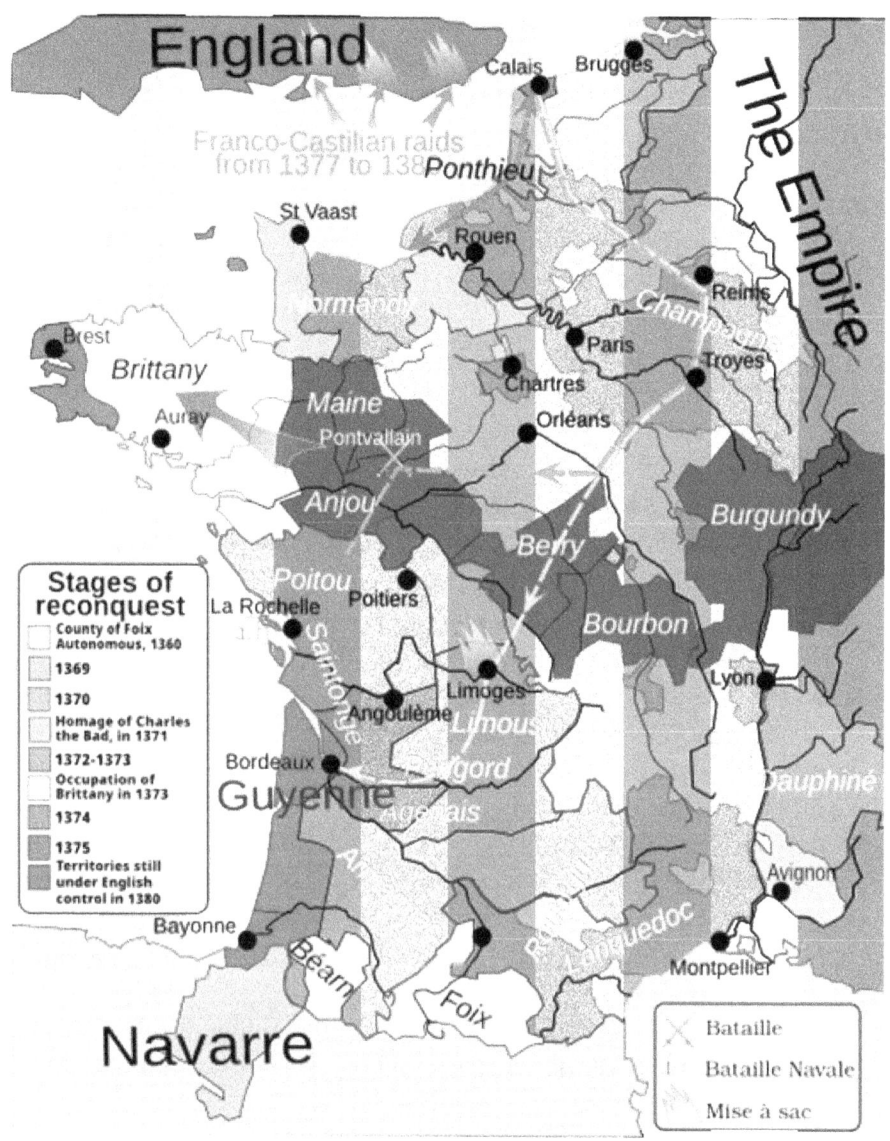

The French recovery of territories.'

The war was continuing to take its toll on the French economy. There was a decline in agricultural production thanks to the chevauchées, and famines were common. Increased taxation added to the burden that the French citizens were carrying, and society was still trying to recover from the Black Death. The Tuchin Revolt (1378-1384) broke out because of the tax burden that workers and artisans were forced to bear. The resistance lasted until the duke of Berry finally suppressed it.

England had to deal with the arrogance and autocracy of Richard II, but France had problems with its monarchy too. The difference was that Richard, for all his faults, was sane. Charles VI was the son of Charles V, and he became king of France in 1380 when he was eleven years old. France was ruled by Philip the Bold, his uncle, while Charles was in his minority. Charles VI took control of the government in 1388, and in the first years of his reign, he was called Charles the Beloved. It appeared that all would be well in the kingdom, but that was not going to happen.

Charles began to suffer fits of madness in the 1390s. There are forty-four separate recorded attacks. The worst one was in 1392 when he attacked his retainers with a sword, killing at least one. Another notable seizure happened in 1393. The king could not remember his name, could not recognize his wife, Queen Isabeau of Bavaria, and did not know he was king. Other attacks included a delusion where he thought he was made of glass. His symptoms suggest that he might have had schizophrenia or bipolar disorder.

Whatever the reason, Charles would have fits of madness followed by periods when he was sane and sober. The fits of insanity disrupted the governance of France, and regencies had to be established when he was not in control of his mental faculties. Factions among the nobles started to rise as the king descended into madness. The Armagnacs and the Burgundians began to quarrel with each other for control of the government. Central authority weakened, and King Charles, despite his bouts of insanity, had a very long reign.[i]

England and France suffered periods of instability during the late 14th century, but the war continued sporadically. It was becoming abundantly clear that temporary treaties would not be a final solution to the problem. One side had to prevail permanently. Either England would have control over France, or France would be an independent nation.

---

[i] New World Encyclopedia.org. (2024, July 19). *Charles VI of France*. Retrieved from Newworldencyclopedia.org: https://www.newworldencyclopedia.org/entry/Charles_VI_of_France

Chapter 7: Henry, Agincourt, and Joan

At the dawn of the 15th century, the Hundred Years' War had been going on for more than sixty years. England still had the upper hand but only by a slight margin. France had suffered disasters in the early days of the war, but it had gained the initiative in the struggle. England, on the other hand, was playing defense most of the time.

Both countries had recovered from the Black Death, but each had also been forced to deal with royal instability. Richard II's arrogance caused internal disturbances, and Charles VI's madness distracted policymakers and military commanders. There had been periods of peace and a few treaties along the way, but the war was still being waged.

Introducing the Bard

William Shakespeare is the greatest English playwright. His comedies and tragedies are performed all over the world. Shakespeare also wrote historical plays. Four of them—Richard II, Henry IV (Parts 1 and 2), and Henry V—are known as the Henriad (some scholars include more plays like Henry VI and Richard III). They cover most of the 15th century of English history. We will be referring to these dramatic works in the following chapters.

We want to remind you that Shakespeare combined fact and fiction in his productions. There is some poetic license, and a few characters are not the people they represent (the real Sir John Falstaff was nothing like the boozy clown in *Henry IV*). However, Shakespeare did not only use his imagination to write the scripts. The playwright used Raphael Holinshed's *Holinshed's Chronicles of England, Scotland, and Ireland* as source material and Edward Hall's *Union of the Two Noble and Illustre Families of Lancaster and York*. Shakespeare did not stray away from those references in his writings. The text he left behind gives us some insight into the motivations of the major players in the latter part of the Hundred Years' War and allows us to understand the political maneuvering that took place better.[i]

England still held a significant amount of land in France in 1400. Its holdings included Aquitaine, the Guyenne region, and the strategically significant seaport of Calais. England was more concerned about holding onto its territory than it was trying to gain more. Its defensive position was a far cry from the days of King Edward III and the Black Prince. The primary English military commanders were John of Gaunt, Duke of Lancaster, and Thomas of Woodstock, Duke of Gloucester. Both were competent soldiers, but they were not of the same caliber as Edward or his son. Additionally, the two men had to deal with the internal politics dominating the reign of Richard II.

By 1400, both John of Gaunt and Thomas of Woodstock were dead. The greatest French commander of the late 14th century was Bertrand du Guesclin. His military successes allowed the French to regain much of the territory that the Treaty of Brétigny had lost. Like his English counterparts, du Guesclin was dead before the end of the 14th century.

---

[i] Rosen, M. (2021, July 14). *The History Behind Shakespeare's Henriad Series*. Retrieved from Leoweekly.com.

Death of Bertrand du Guesclin.[10]

Truce of Leulinghem

Despite their emotional and mental deficiencies, Richard II of England and Charles VI of France were able to negotiate a meaningful truce. Both sides desperately needed a pause in the fighting. England was dealing with internal political divisions and was also on the verge of financial collapse. Charles VI's mental condition restricted the French government's ability to conduct the war.

This truce would end the Caroline phase of the Hundred Years' War. Both parties agreed to it on July 18th, 1389. It was supposed to last three years. However, both monarchs met at Leulinghem and agreed to extend the truce for an additional twenty-seven years.

The truce contained some agreements that were never met. Both countries agreed to start a crusade against the Turks in the Balkans and help bring an end to the Western Schism. The truce included the marriage of Richard to Charles's daughter, Isabella, and that union included a dowry of 800,000 francs. The truce also permitted Portugal and Castile, who were supporting the English and the French, respectively, to lay down their arms and stop fighting.

The truce resulted in the longest sustained peace in the Hundred Years' War. It would last for thirteen years and allow both sides to deal with their domestic problems. Unfortunately, the truce was not a permanent peace. It was rejected by 1402, and the two adversaries were soon back at each other's throats.

Henry Bolingbroke became Henry IV. He was the great king of England, but he was also a usurper. Although Henry could claim royal lineage through his father, everyone knew that he had pulled an anointed king from the throne. Henry would spend his reign defending his right to rule, reminding everyone that he could govern England either from the throne or the saddle of his war horse. A military campaign was launched against Scotland in 1400, but it did not achieve any great results.

Henry's first major challenge came from Wales. Owain Glyndwr led a widespread rebellion against the English Crown, declaring himself prince of Wales in 1400. Despite several military campaigns launched by Henry IV, Glyndwr and his forces controlled much of Wales by 1405, establishing a de facto independent administration and receiving support from both the French and disaffected English nobles.

However, Henry's greatest challenge came from someone he should have been able to trust.

<u>Family Pride</u>

The Percy family was the most powerful northern English family, and its power base was in the county of Northumberland. The English Crown relied upon them to protect the border area against Scottish raids. They supported Henry in his rebellion and provided vital military support that helped him overthrow Richard II. However, the Percys could not be underestimated because their extensive estates generated wealth, and they had the loyalty of many vessels. A prominent Percy was Henry Percy, whose moniker was Hotspur.

King Henry IV appreciated the Percys' help and rewarded them handsomely, but it was insufficient. The Percys claimed they were not adequately compensated for their defense of the Scottish border and that the king had ordered them to hand over their Scottish prisoners instead of allowing them to profit from ransoming them. Another issue was the king's refusal to pay a ransom to release Sir Edmund Mortimer, Hotspur's brother-in-law, from the Welsh.

These grievances might have been resolved through negotiation, but the honor and pride of the Percy family had been deeply wounded. Tensions culminated in open rebellion in 1403, when Henry "Hotspur" Percy raised an army and advanced toward Shrewsbury, hoping to join forces with Welsh rebels and confront the prince of Wales, Henry IV's son. Instead, Percy was met by a royal army under the personal command of Henry IV. The resulting Battle of Shrewsbury was fierce and bloody.

The Battle of Shrewsbury was fought on July 21st, 1403. Both sides used longbowmen, and the sixteen-year-old prince of Wales was seriously wounded by an arrow. Despite the severity of the wound (the arrow pierced his cheekbone), Prince Henry survived. Hotspur was killed, effectively ending the revolt.[i]

King Henry reportedly wept when he was shown Hotspur's body, but when rumors rose that Hotspur was still alive, Henry ordered the dead man's body to be exhumed and quartered, with the parts sent to various cities. Henry Percy was also posthumously declared guilty of high treason. Henry IV demonstrated his ability to assert his authority and caused would-be rebels to think twice about their plans.

Henry's involvement in Wales and against the Percy family occupied much of his time. He focused on maintaining control of the English Channel instead of aggressively campaigning in France. King Henry negotiated a truce in 1407. He used diplomacy instead of combat in his relations with Charles VI. Henry's son was a different story, though.

Warlike Henry

Henry, Prince of Wales, was not quite the spoiled brat portrayed by Shakespeare in *Henry IV, Part 1*. While he did have a very busy social life, Henry took his responsibilities seriously, especially as his father's health gradually declined. He was present at the Battle of Shrewsbury

---

[i] Worldhistory.edu. (2024, February 5). *What Transpired at the Battle of Shrewsbury in 1403*. Retrieved from Worldhistory.edu: https://worldhistoryedu.com/what-transpired-at-the-battle-of-shrewsbury-in-1403/

and fought against the Welsh. His contribution to the English cause was a major factor in the final suppression of the Welsh. By the time young Henry turned his attention to France, he was a battle-tested veteran.[i]

Henry V became the king of England on March 21st, 1413. He was mindful of the challenges his father faced in securing the English throne and the need to consolidate his power as soon as possible. While the nobles pledged their allegiance to him, Henry understood that their loyalty could be fickle. He needed something to occupy the minds of the aristocracy. France provided a tempting opportunity. France was experiencing internal problems and a division between the Armagnac and Burgundian factions. The unpredictable mental condition of the French king added further pressure and made France vulnerable.

Henry had an opportunity to unite the English nobles and the country against a common foe and gain military glory that would enhance his prestige. He was going to take that chance.

Henry V.[ii]

---

[i] Solly, M. (2019, October 31). *The True Story of Henry V, England's Warrior King.* Retrieved from Smithsonianmag.org: https://www.smithsonianmag.com/history/true-story-henry-v-englands-warrior-king-180973432/

The Agincourt Campaign

In the first act of Shakespeare's *Henry V*, the archbishop of Canterbury explains why Henry has a claim to the French throne. It is a lengthy passage, but it underscores the importance of laying out the reasons why Henry believed he had a legitimate right to the throne. Edward III had abandoned his claim to the French throne with the Treaty of Brétigny, but he again made his claim to the French throne once the treaty expired. Henry V was just taking up where his predecessor left off. The French rejected Henry's demand, and war commenced.

Henry's quest for the crown began with the siege of Harfleur. He landed in France with twelve thousand men and began the siege in August 1415. The seaport fell in September, but the English troops were weakened by exhaustion and disease. Henry decided to march to Calais, where his men could rest and regroup.

The French moved to cut him off, assembling an army of over twenty thousand men. Henry only had between six thousand and nine thousand men, but most of them were archers. They were all trained professionals who were not intimidated by French armor. The two sides met on October 25th near the village of Agincourt in northern France. The battle took place on St. Crispin's Day.

The Battle of Agincourt

The battleground was flanked by woods, which limited French movements. Moreover, there had been rain, so the ground was very muddy. The English had their longbows, but their best weapon was the king. Henry V was an inspirational leader who led from the front. His presence in the ranks was a significant motivator, and Henry was an active participant in the fight. Historians estimate that the proportion of English archers was greater than at Crécy or Poitiers.

The topography forced the French to advance through a funnel, and the muddy terrain hampered their movements. English archers fired volleys at the French, causing significant casualties. The final stage of the battle was hand-to-hand combat, with the archers using mallets and swords. It was a crushing defeat for the French, with as many as thirteen thousand casualties. The English suffered only a few hundred.[i]

---

[i] Cartwright, M. (2020, March 2). *Battle of Agincourt*. Retrieved from Worldhistory.org: https://www.worldhistory.org/Battle_of_Agincourt/

The French casualties included three dukes, six counts, ninety barons, the constable of France, and an admiral. Several thousand knights were also dead or wounded.

Henry was a national hero, and he returned to London in November for a processional triumph. The French military leadership was decimated. Henry V conquered Normandy after his 1415 victory at Agincourt and later solidified his position in northern France by allying with Philip the Good, Duke of Burgundy, following the assassination of John the Fearless in 1419. This alliance was crucial to English dominance during the later stages of the Hundred Years' War.

The final event in the chronicle of Henry V's campaigns in France was the Treaty of Troyes. Signed on May 21st, 1420, the treaty stipulated that Henry and his heirs would inherit the French throne upon the death of King Charles VI. Catherine of Valois, the daughter of Charles, was married to Henry, and Henry became the regent of France. It would appear that Henry's victory over the French was complete. However, fate had other plans.[i]

Treaties are creations of diplomacy and political calculation. They can be tedious to read because every possible angle or outcome must be explored and resolved in the text. The Treaty of Troyes was carefully written. No one at the time had any idea of how later circumstances would make that document almost worthless.

Henry V became the regent of France and would succeed Charles VI when the latter died. That succession did not happen, though. Henry died on August 31st, 1422, at the age of thirty-five, and Charles passed away on October 21st of the same year. The Treaty of Troyes stipulated that Henry's infant son would inherit the French throne, but the French contested that claim. They argued that Charles VI was mentally incompetent, so he should not have signed the treaty in the first place. They believed his son, Charles the Dauphin, was the rightful heir despite having been disinherited in the treaty.

This dispute resulted in a power struggle that pitted one section of France against the other. After 1422, the English and their Burgundian allies controlled most of northern France, including territories north of the Loire River. Meanwhile, Charles the Dauphin retained support in

---

[i] History-maps.com. (2024, July 21). *Treaty of Troyes*. Retrieved from History-maps.com: https://history-maps.com/story/Hundred-Years-War/event/Treaty-of-Troyes

southern and central France, especially south of the Loire, which served as the base for his resistance and eventual resurgence.[i]

John the Fearless, Duke of Burgundy, was a pivotal figure of the Hundred Years' War. A rival to the Armagnac faction, which supported the French royal family and the Dauphin Charles (later Charles VII), John positioned himself as both a political player and a military leader. The Burgundians, under his leadership, controlled much of northern and eastern France, including Paris, and often acted independently of—or even in opposition to—the French Crown.

Tensions escalated when John ordered the assassination of Louis, Duke of Orléans, in 1407, accusing him of corrupting the king and mismanaging France. This murder deepened the civil divide between the Armagnacs (supporters of the Dauphin Charles) and the Burgundians. In 1419, in a supposed attempt at reconciliation, John the Fearless met with the Dauphin Charles on the bridge at Montereau. However, the meeting was a trap. John was assassinated by Charles's men.

Outraged by the killing, John's son and successor, Philip the Good, allied with the English, shifting the balance of power in the Hundred Years' War. The Burgundian-English alliance enabled the English to consolidate their hold over northern France.

The Hundred Years' War continued, and the English won several victories, but Henry VI's age was causing some difficulties. There were disputes about how the English should deal with the French and arguments over who would best govern the kingdom while the king was a minor. Events took a significant change in direction by 1429.

An Unforeseen Occurrence

The Hundred Years' War produced commanders of extraordinary military competence. These men rode great horses and wore suits of armor that weighed anywhere from forty to sixty pounds. They performed great feats of military strategy and had amazing victories. It is slightly ironic that the person we know best from that war was a teenage peasant.

Her name was Joan, and she came from a small village named Domrémy. The life she was born into would have been boring, with no greater events than the sunrise and sunset. She could expect to be

---

[i] Britannica, E. o. (2024, July 21). *Charles VI*. Retrieved from Britannica.com: https://www.britannica.com/biography/Charles-VI-king-of-France

married before she was twenty, have several pregnancies, and might live into her forties or fifties, provided she did not die giving birth. Destiny had other plans for this young girl.

Joan claimed that she heard voices from Saint Michael, Saint Catherine, and Saint Margaret. These saints directed her to support the Dauphin Charles and throw the English out of France. Somehow, Joan summoned the courage to convince a local army officer to help her get to Chinon, where Charles was in residence. There, Joan convinced Charles that God had sent her to save France.

It seems incredible that Charles agreed to allow the teenage girl to lead his armies against the battle-tested English. That by itself was a miracle. Joan firmly believed in her mission and had the charisma to sway people, including Yolande of Aragon, the Dauphin's mother-in-law. An examination conducted by theologians and church officials concluded that Joan was not a heretic or deceitful. Charles even had a private conversation with Joan, where she revealed information that only Charles knew. This convinced Charles to give the military command to Joan. There was also a practical reason—Charles had nothing to lose.

A Desperate Move

The French were in dire straits. England controlled much of northern France and had the city of Orléans under siege. The fall of that city would be a significant blow to Charles and his aspirations. The French military leadership had not delivered any results, and the rank-and-file soldiers were demoralized. Joan might be the person who could improve matters. Charles believed it was worth a chance.

On the Offensive

Orléans had been under siege since October 1428, and there was a good chance that the city would fall. Charles gave Joan a small army, and she moved toward Orléans on April 27th, 1429. Joan's forces had to deal with several English strongholds. She took the first fort on May 4th. She then attacked another fort on May 6th and succeeded in taking it.

On May 7th, an invigorated French army advanced against the English fort at Les Tourelles. Joan was wounded in the ensuing battle, but the French fought until the English surrendered. The English retreated from Orléans on May 8th. Joan had successfully lifted the siege, and French morale among the soldiers and the common people skyrocketed.[i]

---

[i] Yvonne Lanhers, M. G. (2024, June 5). *St. Joan of Arc*. Retrieved from Britannica.com:

Joan kept up the pressure on the English and won several victories in the following weeks. She did not actually fight in the battles, but she inspired the soldiers and helped outline the military strategy they would follow. The culmination of her efforts occurred on July 17th, 1429, when Charles was crowned Charles VII in Reims, legitimizing him in the eyes of the people.[i]

Fortune Shifted

Joan had accomplished her mission of having Charles crowned, but she was still motivated by ridding France of the English. Unfortunately, her streak of good luck ended abruptly.

The Burgundians captured Joan during the siege of Compiègne in May 1430 and sold her to the English. Charles did not try to ransom her. The English were probably not willing to give up someone who had become a rallying point for the French people anyway. Joan was taken to Rouen in December, and she was placed on trial for heresy.

The Trial and Execution

The proceedings of Joan's trial were documented and provide a considerable amount of information about her. These records and the investigation in the 1450s provide insight into the trial and how the English manipulated everything. Joan was interrogated on February 21st, 1431, and these sessions lasted until March 17th. Joan was questioned about everything regarding her role and her supernatural connections. The official trial began on March 26th. Joan was pressured into signing a document where she renounced her visions and agreed to no longer wear men's clothes. However, Joan recanted on May 28th and donned men's clothing again. She was sentenced to be executed. Joan of Arc was burned at the stake on May 30th, 1431.

---

https://www.britannica.com/biography/Saint-Joan-of-Arc

[i] Editors, H. (2018, August 21). *Siege of Orleans.* Retrieved from History.com: https://www.history.com/topics/middle-ages/siege-of-orleans

Joan of Arc.[12]

Her death did not mean that the English were rid of her. Instead, Joan became an even greater rallying point for the French people, as they viewed her as a martyr. She galvanized popular support in favor of Charles and provided a focal point for national unity. Years later, an ecclesiastical tribunal was conducted, and the original verdict was overturned because it was biased. Joan was canonized as a saint on May 16th, 1920, and she is the patron saint of France.

Joan of Arc's story is a fascinating tale. She continues to amaze people and reminds us that young girls could play a significant role in making history. Historians and other scholars continue to examine and speculate about the life of the Maid of Orléans. There are two questions we are going to explore.

Did Charles VII Abandon Joan?

Charles owed his coronation to Joan of Arc. It is puzzling that he made no effort to ransom or get her back after the enemy captured her.

To begin with, medieval court politics was a cutthroat business. The royal favorite was envied and hated by other courts who wanted the king's attention. No doubt, Joan had enemies in the French court who were jealous of her. While they might not have actively plotted against her, they were ready to take advantage when Joan slipped. Those courtiers might have convinced Charles VII that Joan was no longer useful and that there was no reason to spend large amounts of money ransoming her.

Charles VII is remembered for being a very astute politician and diplomat. He might have decided on his own that Joan was becoming a liability or that she was no longer needed by him to maintain his throne. Modern readers may consider either decision to be cold-blooded, but a monarch ruling at that time rarely had the luxury of being a compassionate figure.

Was Joan of Arc Insane?

Joan's claims of hearing voices and seeing visions have generated curiosity about her mental condition. Were these signs of schizophrenia or some other mental disorder? Contemporaries of Joan have commented on her overall intelligence. She might have been an illiterate peasant girl, but she had a remarkable understanding of the law, and her memory was excellent. These contemporaries were not avid followers of Joan but rather physicians who had experience dealing with mental illness.

The royal family had experience in dealing with someone who was mentally disturbed. If Joan had shown signs of being mentally unstable, she would have been dismissed as mad and sent back home. Charles VII was risking his future and his reputation in placing his confidence in Joan.[i]

---

[i] Cremer Consulting. (2019, July 8). *Did Joan of Arc Suffer From Mental Illness?* Retrieved from

One possible explanation is that Joan might have been the victim of a type of epilepsy. Dr. Giuseppe d'Orsi, a neurologist, and Paola Tinuper, an associate professor of biomedical and neuromotor sciences at the University of Bologna, have presented the hypothesis that Joan suffered from a form of epilepsy known as idiopathic epilepsy with auditory features. The trial records provide evidence of symptoms that suggest Joan had this disability, which explains the auditory and visual hallucinations. However, this explanation is a hypothesis. DNA samples would have to be examined to determine if Joan had epilepsy.[i]

Whatever her psychological condition might have been, there is no denying that Joan succeeded where experienced military commanders had failed. Her participation in the Hundred Years' War was a dramatic turning point. France was now clearly gaining the upper hand. The days of the English presence in France were coming to an end.

Cremerconsulting.com: https://www.cremerconsulting.com/en/did-joan-of-arc-suffer-from-mental-illness/

[i] Miller, S. G. (2016, July 29). *What Really Caused the Voices in Joan of Arc's Head?* Retrieved from Livescience.com: https://www.livescience.com/55597-joan-of-arc-voices-epilepsy.html

Chapter 8: Culture of the Hundred Years' War

The 14th and 15th centuries saw the beginning of the greatest cultural movement Western civilization had ever seen: the Renaissance. Northern Italian cities such as Florence produced masters in the arts whose work continues to amaze us.

The modern reader must understand that the changes were not restricted to Italy. Other places experienced growth in the arts as well. Culture flourished despite the war. Even though men were fighting and dying on battlefields, painters were producing masterpieces, poets were writing rhymes that we still quote, and writers created incredibly beautiful and compelling prose. Northern Europe, which includes England and France, also experienced a renaissance and produced its own masters.

The Burgundian Court

Burgundy was as important to the development of art in the 15th century as Florence. The court of the dukes of Burgundy was a magnet for some of the greatest artists of the period, and the rulers of Burgundy were very influential patrons. Burgundian influence on art started with Philip the Bold in the late 14th century. The wealth that the dukes acquired from the textile trade and wine industry permitted them to have a visually magnificent court culture. Philip the Good actively promoted the visual arts. One master artist who prospered under his patronage was Jan van Eyck.[i]

---

[i] Wisse, J. (2002, October). *Burgundian Netherlands: Private Life.* Retrieved from

Art historian and Renaissance painter Giorgio Vasari claimed that van Eyck invented oil painting. That is probably not true, but this Flemish artist did paint art that was rich in color and had a high degree of naturalism. The richness of the color of his work is exemplified in works such as *The Arnolfini Portrait* and *Portrait of a Man*, the latter of which is believed to be a self-portrait. How he produced the paint that produced such lush color remains a mystery. It was rumored that the artist was part alchemist. Modern art researchers are still trying to determine his recipe for the paint.[i]

The Arnolfini Portrait by Jan van Eyck.[18]

Metmuseum.org: https://www.metmuseum.org/toah/hd/bnpr/hd_bnpr.htm

[i] Theartstory.org. (2024, July 22). *Summary of Jan Van Eyck*. Retrieved from Theartstory.org: https://www.theartstory.org/artist/van-eyck-jan/

We know that van Eyck created depth of color in his work by using a wet-on-wet technique. Van Eyck would add layers of wet paint before the previous layers had dried. This allowed him to blend the colors and create a three-dimensional image on his canvas. He would also use translucent glaze to accentuate the richness of the figures.[i]

Van Eyck also used heat-bodied linseed oil for texture and was willing to use very expensive ingredients for his paint. The ultramarine he used for *Portrait of a Man* was a blue chaperon made by using lapis lazuli, which explains the intensity of the blue.[ii]

Portrait of a Man. This is believed to be a self-portrait.[14]

---

[i] Cole, M. (2020, August 9). *How to Decipher the Symbolism in Jan Van Eyck's Famous "Arnolfini Portrait."* Retrieved from Mymodernmet.com: https://mymodernmet.com/arnolfini-portrait/

[ii] Focusonbelgium.be. (2015, October 13). *Did You Know That Oil Painting Was Invented By the Belgian Van Eyck Brothers?* Retrieved from Focusonbelgium.be: https://focusonbelgium.be/en/facts/did-you-know-oil-painting-was-invented-belgian-van-eyck-brothers

Van Eyck did more than paint portraits. He painted decorations and also painted religious artwork for churches.

We are indebted to the generosity of the Burgundian dukes who enabled gifted masters like van Eyck to ply their trade and develop even greater expertise. We have the privilege of viewing these great pieces of art in museums all over the world.

Architecture

Architecture in the late 14th and early 15th centuries was primarily concerned with completing existing projects. Gothic cathedrals, whose construction might have started in the 12th or 13th century, were finished.

The completed churches were magnificent. The Beauvais Cathedral had a spire that reached 153 meters high, and the Great East Window of Gloucester Cathedral is one of the largest examples of stained-glass art in Britain. The Canterbury Cathedral's Bell Harry Tower was completed in the late 15th century. York Minster, one of the largest Gothic cathedrals in northern Europe, had extensive work done during the 14th and 15th centuries. The Chapter House is octagonal and is known for its wooden vaulting and elaborate stone carvings. Its design is one of the reasons why York Minster is a UNESCO World Heritage Site.

The Chapter House.[15]

A unique cathedral construction project completed in the 15th century was the Butter Tower of the Rouen Cathedral. The project was funded by donations from parishioners who, in exchange for contributing money to the effort, were allowed to eat butter during Lent.

The Extravagance of the Popes

The papacy can be justifiably criticized for what happened during the 14th and 15th centuries. Its turn away from spirituality to extravagance undermined the church's role as a moral force in society and led to dramatic problems that were not resolved by the start of the 16th century. However, it also has to be recognized that the popes were lavish patrons of the arts, and culture flourished because of their generosity.

The most significant architectural achievement of the Avignon Papacy was the Palais des Papes. Pope Benedict XII was forced to accept that Avignon would be the papal residence. He decided that it needed a palace suitable for the pope. He chose to build this palace on the site of the bishop's palace in the city, compensating the current bishop with the residence of a deceased cardinal.

Pierre-Marie Poisson was selected as the architect, and work started on the palace in 1335. Poisson was assisted by Jean du Louvres, and it took less than twenty years to build the palace. Pope Clement VI would later add an additional building to the Palais des Papes.[1]

When it was completed, it was the largest Gothic building in Europe. The Palais des Papes housed the papal library, which had over two thousand volumes. The ornamental work inside includes incredible frescoes, especially in the Saint-Martial Chapel. Another notable work of interior art is the frescoes of the prophets that adorn the vault of the great audience chamber.

The Palais des Papes was a magnet for culture. Luminaries of the time, such as Petrarch, were drawn to this papal residence. Musicians and composers were also welcome. The Avignon Papacy supported manuscript illumination, which was noted for its intricate design and vibrant colors.

The cultural exchange taking place in the Palais des Papes and in Avignon made a significant contribution to the culture of Europe. Cultural ideas were exchanged among the artists and scholars who came

---

[1] Spottinghistory.com. (2024, July 22). *Palais des Papes*. Retrieved from Spottinghistory.com: https://www.spottinghistory.com/view/6387/palais-des-papes/

from all parts of Europe. There was a cross-pollination of arts that enriched Western civilization. Scholarship was important to the popes, and treatises on Christian doctrine and philosophy were produced during the "Babylonian Captivity." No one can deny the contributions of the French popes at Avignon. The Palais des Papes is a UNESCO World Heritage Site and draws thousands of people annually.[i]

The Palais des Papes[16]

Evolution of Language

We often concentrate on the visual and performing arts when discussing culture, but other areas also merit attention. The 15th century saw a dramatic cultural transition in the spoken and written word. This evolution involved a renewed interest in Latin and a growing emphasis on the proper use of the vernacular language. Standardized forms of speech were replacing dialects in conversation and writing.

Dante Alighieri, an Italian poet, was a pioneer in the development of the Italian language in the late 13th and 14th centuries. His *Divine Comedy* proved that the vernacular could express complex themes. Petrarch, another Italian poet, followed his lead. He is considered the Father of Humanism, and he wrote in Latin and the vernacular as well. His writings hinted that Tuscan was a suitable means of written expression.

Tuscan became the dialect of preference for other Italian writers. Giovanni Boccaccio wrote *The Decameron* in the Tuscan dialect. This work demonstrates the richness and flexibility of Tuscan-based Italian. Drawing on the study of Latin grammar, scholars in Italy started using

---

[i] Palais-des-papes.com. (2024, July 22). *Priceless Frescoes.* Retrieved from Palais-des-papes.com: https://palais-des-papes.com/des-fresques-inestimables/

syntactical structures, which created greater regularity in written Italian and also a higher level of sophistication. They were elevating Italian into a linguistic form that was just as refined as classical Latin.[i]

The Power of Words

King Henry IV did something revolutionary at his coronation. He addressed the congregation in English, not French. Henry considered himself an English monarch. He saw England as not just one of his territorial holdings but his mother country.[ii]

French had been the spoken word of the courts of law, the royal court, and elite society since the Norman conquest. Middle English was something that the common people spoke. Gradually, the use of language shifted away from French to a modified form of English that had French words in it, but the base was essentially Germanic. A major step forward was the Statute of Pleading, which was enacted in 1362. This established English as the language of the courts of law.

Greater things were soon to follow. English was being used in daily communications and literature. The greatest work of English literature before the Elizabethan era was not written in Latin or French but in a form of common English.

Geoffrey Chaucer: Father of English Literature

Geoffrey Chaucer was a Renaissance man long before the term became popular. He served in the Hundred Years' War, was captured by the French, and was ransomed by King Edward III. He would serve as a diplomat and a bureaucrat in the English government.

Chaucer was a man of many talents, but what he is most famous for is what he did with the quill in his hand.[iii] Chaucer was a gifted writer. One of his early works was *The House of Fame*, which was influenced by a mission to Italy, where he read Petrarch and Boccaccio. *Troilus and Criseyde*, another poem, is considered his finest work.

---

[i] Strachan, D. (2024, July 22). *La Lingua Toscana: Tuscany's Dialect and the Birth of Italian.* Retrieved from Tuscanynowandmre.com: https://www.tuscanynowandmore.com/discover-italy/history/italian-language-tuscan-dialect

[ii] Kingscoronation.com. (2024, July 22). *Coronation of Henry IV.* Retrieved from Kingscoronation.com: https://kingscoronation.com/coronation-henry-iv/

[iii] Lumiansky, R. (2024, May 30). *Geoffrey Chaucer Diplomat and Civil Servant.* Retrieved from Britannica.com: https://www.britannica.com/biography/Geoffrey-Chaucer/Diplomat-and-civil-servant

Chaucer took time from his official duties to write, and his contributions to English are significant. At the time, French or Latin were the languages writers and scholars used in England, making Chaucer a revolutionary. He used the decasyllabic couplet, a rhyme scheme where each stanza has four lines with ten syllables. He used this composition in his most famous work, *The Canterbury Tales*. Chaucer also used an iambic pentameter to craft his verses.[i]

His greatest gift, however, was the use of vernacular English. Chaucer elevated English to a higher status and proved it could be used for significant literary expression. English was more than just the voice of the common people. In *The Canterbury Tales*, Chaucer shows the richness of the English language. *The Canterbury Tales* provides a multilayered narrative and demonstrates that English can meet that type of literary challenge. Chaucer proved that English was able to present different literary styles and themes effectively. It was so much more than the grunts and snorts of a peasant.

We suspect there was a little bit of the entrepreneurial businessman in Geoffrey Chaucer. Texts written in Latin could only be read by highly educated people, which meant that only a select audience could appreciate an author's efforts. Chaucer was writing for the middle class, people who might not be able to read Latin but could read English. This meant his audience was much larger than what the ordinary court poet might reach. His example encouraged other English poets and writers to dare to use ordinary words. Writing in English also helped his fellow citizens form a national identity and a sense of pride in their mother tongue.

Chaucer was not the only writer who dared to go off the beaten track. John Lydgate also wrote in English, and Thomas Malory, author of *Le Morte d'Arthur*, added his work to the growing catalog of prose and literature written in English. The English language benefited from the revival of interest in Latin. Latin words entered the English vocabulary during the 15th century, and Latin grammar influenced the development of writing styles. It was not long before a successful transition from Middle to Early Modern English happened.

---

[i] Poets.org. (2024, July 22). *Geoffrey Chaucer*. Retrieved from Poets.org: https://poets.org/poet/geoffrey-chaucer

Other Writers

Italian and English were not the only languages that changed during the Hundred Years' War. Jean Froissart, a French author, did more than write a history of the 14th century. He was also a poet, and his narrative poems helped educate the French about court life. He was willing to use the language of the day instead of relying only on Latin.

An interesting French writer of the time was Christine de Pizan. She is one of the first women to work as a professional writer. She would be considered a feminist today because she advocated for women's equality in her writings. She did not hesitate to challenge the male-dominated world of letters, and her work was extremely popular, so much so that it was translated into other languages.[i]

All these cultural developments occurred as the Hundred Years' War continued. However, by the 1430s, events suggested that there was going to be an end to all of the fighting. The final days of combat were coming into view, and the English were starting to look more like losers than winners.

---

[i] Mark, J. J. (2019, March 26). *Christine de Pizan.* Retrieved from Worldhistory.org: https://www.worldhistory.org/Christine_de_Pizan/

Chapter 9: The Collapse of English Power

The English had burned the Maid of Orléans and hoped that would end the problem. It did not. Instead of being demoralized by the heroine's death, the French were energized. Joan of Arc became a martyr to France, which roused the public. Even worse, the English were required to deal with a phenomenon they had not had to be concerned about for years: a competent French king. Charles VII was not his father's son at all. Despite being disinherited by the Treaty of Troyes and humiliated by French failures, Charles was a pragmatic individual. He was willing to be patient and rebuild his power base. He looked for opportunities to succeed where others had failed. Charles was going to be a very difficult enemy for the English.

<u>Taking the Initiative</u>

Charles understood he was not the warrior King Edward III of England had been. He trusted his commanders to perform their jobs, and his trust in Joan of Arc was incredible, especially given that Joan had no prior military experience.

The Loire Campaign was the high mark of Joan of Arc's military career. Assisted by Jehn II, Duke of Alençon, Joan systematically took back the Loire Valley from the English. She defeated the English in several battles, notably the Battle of Patay, which took place on June 18th, 1429. The French ambushed the English and attacked from various directions. A larger English army under the command of Sir John

Falstaff was defeated, and many of the veteran English commanders were killed or captured. It was a decisive victory for France and had very serious consequences that went beyond losing the contest on the field.

The Battle of Patay.[17]

Charles was not a knight in shining armor doing brave deeds on the battlefield. Such exploits had not helped French kings in the past. Charles was a very good diplomat and a shrewd politician. What he did behind the scenes proved more valuable to France than any cavalry charge.

Negotiating with the Burgundians

A trouble spot was the relations France had with Burgundy. The duchy was a significant ally of England and posed a threat to the north and west of France. The trouble with Burgundy started with the assassination of Duke John the Fearless. Charles had to make things right. He reached out to the Burgundians and sent his best negotiators to talk with the current duke, Philip the Good. The result of the negotiations was the Treaty of Arras, signed on September 21st, 1435.

Charles condemned the murderers of John the Fearless and promised to punish them. In return, Philip the Good recognized Charles as the rightful king of France. Philip demanded that he be exempted from paying homage to the crown, and Charles agreed. The homage would be resumed after either Charles or Philip died.

One important consequence of the treaty was that the alliance between England and Burgundy was finished. Charles no longer had to worry about a second front with Burgundy and concentrated more on dealing with the English. It also meant that France was in a stronger position than before.[i]

A Reforming Monarch

There were some changes that France needed to make in order to become a stronger nation, and Charles was more than willing to push through the reforms. The king was no longer content with relying on feudal levies to raise troops for military campaigns. Charles established France's first permanent standing army in more than a thousand years. The professional soldiers would be an essential part of the reconquest of Normandy, which Charles was able to do in the 1440s.

The army needed money, and Charles was interested in stabilizing the finances of his kingdom. He successfully acquired the permanent right to levy taxes. The taille, a direct land tax, gave him a steady source of revenue.

Charles VII worked to strengthen the central administration of his kingdom. In 1438, the king issued the Pragmatic Sanction of Bourges, which limited papal authority over the French church and gave Charles authority over ecclesiastical revenues.[ii]

Charles did face challenges as a monarch, including several revolts. Nevertheless, he proved to be one of the best kings of France and rightfully earned the moniker Charles the Victorious. His success and his ability to rule were in sharp contrast to the English Crown, which was undergoing severe tension and distress in the mid-15th century.

England had been blessed in the Late Middle Ages with decisive kings who had excellent leadership skills. Regrettably, these men were succeeded by weak and ineffective monarchs. Edward I was followed by Edward II, Edward III was succeeded by Richard II, and Henry V was succeeded by Henry VI. Three of these men were disasters, and each one was eventually murdered.

---

[i] Longueville, O. (202, September 25). *The Treaty of Arras of 1435: The End of the Civil Strife in France.* Retrieved from Olivialongueville.com: https://olivialongueville.com/2020/09/25/the-treaty-of-arras-of-1435-the-end-of-the-civil-strife-in-france/

[ii] Lanhers, Y. (2024, July 18). *Charles VII.* Retrieved from Britannica.com: https://www.britannica.com/biography/Charles-VII-king-of-France

A significant issue was age. Richard II and Henry VI were children (in the case of Henry VI, a baby) when they assumed the throne. England was governed by regents for extended periods of time. These advisors were often corrupt and interested in their own advancement and acquisition of wealth rather than good governance. Their inability to govern well created situations that destabilized the authority of the crown.

A Sad Story

Shakespeare's *Henry VI* tells the tale of a well-meaning but weak monarch. Henry VI was profoundly religious and more inclined to pray than govern. His piety was commendable, but he was not like his father at all. Henry V was charismatic and could command men; his son had trouble making firm decisions. The poor character of his advisors made things worse.

Humphrey of Lancaster, Duke of Gloucester

Humphrey of Lancaster, Duke of Gloucester, was young Henry's uncle and served as the lord protector of England from 1422 to 1437. The duke participated in Henry V's campaigns and fought at Agincourt, but he was not a military figure. He had an intellectual upbringing and was a highly cultured individual. The duke of Gloucester was a patron of learning and gave generous donations to the University of Oxford. Unfortunately, he was impulsive and unscrupulous.

Duke Humphrey's library at Oxford. [18]

His brother, John, Duke of Bedford, was in charge of military operations in France, while Humphrey was heavily involved in domestic and diplomatic affairs. Humphrey wanted to assert English dominance and was a nationalist at heart. While he was popular with the English public, he quarreled bitterly with both his brother and his uncle, Cardinal Henry Beaufort.

The cardinal was a prince of the church (a term historically used to refer to cardinals in the Catholic Church) and also a papal legate. In addition to that, he served as lord chancellor of England. He was as interested in temporal affairs as he was in spiritual matters, and frequently, the former took priority over the latter. Humphrey did not approve of that and felt that his uncle had no right to interfere in domestic policy. Cardinal Henry Beaufort was incredibly wealthy, though, and he used his money to provide loans to the state at high interest rates. The rivalry between Humphrey and Beaufort for power caused them to argue frequently, which was a distraction. England needed sound governance during Henry's minority, not two relatives bickering.[i]

Humphrey also had a rough relationship with John, Duke of Bedford. John was the regent of France and was in charge of conducting the war. Humphrey wanted an aggressive military strategy and was constantly preparing for a fight. John was pragmatic and willing to use diplomacy to attain his objectives.

Humphrey did not get along well with the Burgundians, which was a severe problem. Burgundy was an influential ally of the English, and John was trying to maintain good relations with the duchy. Humphrey had a dispute with the duke of Burgundy that involved Humphrey's wife and her inheritance. He began a private war that created a serious divide. Events came to a head when John died in 1435. Philip the Good was tired of dealing with Humphrey, and their animosity was what led to the Treaty of Arras. Burgundy switched sides, and England lost a valuable ally.

---

[i] Britannica, E. o. (2024, July 30). *Henry Beaufort*. Retrieved from Britannica.com: https://www.britannica.com/biography/Henry-Beaufort

The Noble Witch

A fascinating story during this time involved Eleanor Cobham, Duchess of Gloucester. She was initially Humphrey's mistress, and the duke married her after his first marriage was absolved by the pope. Eleanor was ambitious and made enemies at court for her grand style.

In 1441, Eleanor was accused of necromancy. It seems that two of her acquaintances had been arrested for casting a horoscope that predicted Henry VI was going to die soon. That was an act of treason, and Eleanor was implicated. Although she denied the charge of treason, Eleanor admitted that she had used the services of Margery Jourdemayne, who was a well-known witch. The duchess was eventually found guilty of witchcraft, but she was not burned at the stake. Instead, she performed public penance and was imprisoned for life in Chester Castle. This did not mean Eleanor was in a dark cell in the basement. She actually had a staff.[i]

The scandal surrounding his wife Eleanor's conviction for sorcery and treason in 1441 had deeply embarrassed Humphrey, prompting his withdrawal from public life. However, his political influence and royal lineage still made him a threat to powerful factions at court. On February 20th, 1447, just before a session of Parliament, Humphrey was arrested on a charge of treason, though no formal trial or evidence followed. He died three days later, likely from a stroke. His uncle, Cardinal Henry Beaufort, died a few weeks later on April 11th, 1447.

Two Royal Favorites

Henry VI cannot be blamed for the mistakes made when he was still a boy. However, his ability to govern did not improve as he grew older. The king had incredibly poor political judgment, and he could not effectively manage the rivalries of the English nobility.

Henry was declared fit to rule in 1437, but this did not mean that he was competent to reign. The young man was deeply religious, but he had a timid nature. He relied on stronger men to govern England, which was a terrible mistake.

William de la Pole was the earl of Suffolk and a military commander who served well during the early French campaigns of Henry V. He was

---

[i] Hayle, J. (2022, December 22). *Accused: A Royal Witch in Medieval England.* Retrieved from Hubpages.com: https://discover.hubpages.com/education/Eleanor-Duchess-of-Gloucester-Medieval-Royal-Accused-of-Witchcraft

the principal negotiator of the marriage between Henry VI and Margaret of Anjou, Charles VII's niece, in 1444. He was rewarded by being promoted to the marquess of Suffolk. William (commonly referred to as Suffolk) was one of Henry's closest advisors and influenced many of the monarch's decisions and policies. However, his control of royal favor caused other nobles to resent him, particularly Richard, Duke of York.

An illustration of Suffolk and Margaret in Henry VI.[19]

Suffolk's role in negotiating the Treaty of Tours, which was signed on May 28th, 1444, and securing Henry VI's marriage to Margaret of Anjou would later bring him severe political trouble. As part of the agreement, England secretly agreed to return the province of Maine to France, a clause that was not publicly disclosed at the time. Although the treaty established a two-year truce in the Hundred Years' War, which was later extended, many in England viewed the concessions as humiliating once they were revealed. Suffolk was blamed for surrendering English interests and was seen as complicit in a weak and costly peace, contributing to his eventual downfall.[1]

Internal politics in England were causing challenges for the English military effort in France. There was also a crisis in military leadership that became more pronounced with each passing year. In 1430, England had tight control over most of northern France; this control evaporated by 1453. The English military was not as invincible as it once was.

The Disaster at Patay

A notable shift in momentum was beginning to occur. It had started with the raising of the siege of Orléans and the death of Thomas Montague, Earl of Salisbury, commander of the English forces at Orléans. Now, the French were beginning to become more aggressive, winning battles and taking back territory.

We often consider the commanders when we review the battles. Yet, what wins the fight is not necessarily a charismatic leader urging his troops forward. Instead, the commanders of the various units often determine the final outcome. The men who lead the companies and battle divisions see to it that commands are executed precisely, and when opportunities arise on the field, they lead men into the breach to secure the victories. The most significant loss the English suffered at Patay was the field commanders who were killed or captured by the French. Their battle-tested leadership was gone, and they were replaced by less experienced and less capable officers. The brainpower England needed within the military ranks was now missing.

Charles took advantage of the power vacuum in the English army. The French were able to regain significant amounts of territory south, east, and north of Paris.

The Fall of Paris

John, Duke of Bedford, was a competent general and a very astute diplomat. He understood the importance of alliances and how other people expected to be treated. Burgundy's presence in northern and western France caused the French to pause before they mounted any significant offensive against the English in the east.

---

[1] Medievalhistory.info. (2024, July 30). *The Treaty of Tours-Peace in Our Time*. Retrieved from Medievalhistory.info: https://medievalhistory.info/the-treaty-of-tours-peace-in-out-time-1444/

That changed after he died. Humphrey, Duke of Gloucester, permitted his petty squabbles with Burgundy to overshadow maintaining a good rapport. He practically pushed Philip the Good into the arms of the French as a result. The loss of Burgundy as an ally continued a downward spiral for the English.

Charles pressed his advantage after the Treaty of Arras was signed. Burgundy was no longer a military threat, and the French were successful in gradually taking over the English fortifications surrounding Paris. The English could not get the necessary supplies and reinforcements, and by April 6th, 1436, they were forced back inside the city walls. The English finally surrendered Paris on April 17th, 1436, and the garrison was allowed to withdraw from the city.

The siege of Paris.[20]

The fall of Paris meant more than weakening the English in northern France. King Charles VII's legitimacy was now confirmed, and the morale of the French was boosted dramatically. The road to final victory was becoming more apparent, and Charles was not turning back.

The Advantage of Technology

The longbow was a primary advantage for the English in the 14th century. In the 15th century, the French would use technological advances to gain success, and they excelled in artillery. Early cannons were not very reliable and were prone to exploding. The French made advancements in cannon design, using better casting and creating more accurate artillery pieces. The French used bombards, culverins, and mortars. These neutralized the effectiveness of the English longbow. The new artillery also made English fortifications vulnerable and nearly useless.

The psychological effect of artillery fire cannot be denied. A combination of loud explosions and destructive power caused panic within the English ranks. French artillery increasingly became a deciding factor. It was the key to the success of the French during the Norman Campaign.

Small cannons and a hand culverin from the 15th century.[n]

The Disaster of Tours

The English proved themselves to be bungling fools in diplomacy. The Treaty of Tours surrendered Maine to the French without a fight. A glance at the map of France can tell anyone how important this province was to English holdings in northern France. Both Maine and Anjou were buffer zones protecting Normandy, and giving up this territory compromised the English defense of its territories. Additionally, the fortresses held in Maine and Anjou protected needed supply lines. The Treaty of Tours was not well received by the English people, and soldiers in the field considered it a betrayal. The French now had a direct line into Normandy.

The Norman Campaign

The truce provided by the Treaty of Tours provided a temporary relief in the fighting and gave France a chance to plan and prepare its forces for an offensive against Normandy. Rouen, the capital of Normandy, fell in 1449, and the French won a decisive victory at Formigny on April 15th, 1450. The last important English force in Normandy was destroyed in that battle, and English Normandy felt like a house of cards. Caen was lost to France on June 12th, 1450, and the English lost Cherbourg on August 12th, 1450. Normandy was now permanently French.

The siege of Cherbourg.[22]

To make matters worse, there were years of fiscal chaos in England. The nation had taken out substantial loans to finance campaigns, and these obligations had high interest rates attached to them. There was a decline in royal income because of an economic slump. The duke of Suffolk had tried to solve the problem by raising taxes, but his pleas to Parliament to authorize tax increases were denied. Suffolk was already being blamed for the Treaty of Tours, and the financial troubles were only adding to the accusations. Eventually, he was charged with treason and tried to flee. The ship he was on was intercepted in the English

Channel, and the former royal favorite was executed by the other ship's crew on May 2nd, 1450.[i]

Normandy was now safely in the hands of the French, and the kingdom could turn its attention to the last English holdings in the country. Southwestern France had been English property for over three hundred years. It was going to change ownership permanently.

France took Bordeaux in 1451, but on October 23rd, 1452, John Talbot, Earl of Shrewsbury, took the city back. The English had the upper hand in southwestern France, but it was a temporary success. Charles VII was determined to take control of Aquitaine.

The Battle of Castillon

The pivotal battle took place at Castillon on July 17th, 1453. Castillon was an English-held town that was being besieged by a large French army. Talbot was waiting in Bordeaux to get more reinforcements, but he decided to march out to relieve the garrison of the besieged town. The French, under Jean Bureau, had constructed a well-defended camp outside of Castillon. Bureau created an artillery park that consisted of a deep trench and an earthen wall that was reinforced by tree trunks. The park had as many as three hundred guns of various sizes.

Talbot and the English army arrived and defeated a small French detachment of archers. Boosted by this quick victory, the English misread what they thought was a French retreat and advanced. They ran into a superior French force. The English ranks were decimated by the cannon fire. Talbot was killed in the struggle, and the arrival of Breton cavalry forced the English to retreat. Most of the English army was killed or captured on that day, and what was left surrendered on July 19th. The defeat resulted in the English losing any remaining control they had over southwestern France. Bordeaux was retaken on October 19th.

Technology significantly changed the outcome of the battle. The lethal longbow had been replaced by field artillery. The French won because they had the better guns.

---

[i] Medievalhistory.info. (2024, July 30). *How England Lost the Hundred Years' War*. Retrieved from Medievalhistory.info: https://medievalhistory.info/how-england-lost-the-hundred-years-war

The death of John Talbot.[38]

The King Is Mad, Part Two

France endured a period when the king was insane, and England was about to experience the same. King Henry VI suffered what appeared to be a nervous breakdown in August 1453 when he learned of the defeat at Castillon. What was frightening about this is that the mental collapse was so severe that the king became unresponsive and did not react to the news of his son's birth.

Henry might have been predisposed toward mental illness because of genetics. His maternal grandfather was King Charles VI of France, and his mother, Catherine of Valois, suffered from bouts of mental instability. Schizophrenia or bipolar disorder could have caused Henry's emotional and mental collapse. Whatever the reason was, the English king was incapacitated.[i]

---

[i] Hughes, T. (2019, March 11). *What Were the Incidents of King Henry VI's Illness?* Retrieved from Historyhit.com: https://www.historyhit.com/what-were-the-incidents-of-king-henry-vis-madness/

England was in a horrific state as the summer of 1453 came to an end. It had lost its best field commander, it was in a horrible financial state, and what was left of England's possessions in France was Calais. Nevertheless, England was reluctant to swallow its pride and formally call an end to the war.

Chapter 10: The End of the Fighting

The official end of the Hundred Years' War was the Treaty of Picquigny, signed on August 29th, 1475, between King Edward IV of England and King Louis XI of France. Both sides agreed to settle future differences through negotiation instead of military action. There was no formal peace treaty; however, 1453 is still considered the end date of the Hundred Years' War. There are several reasons for this.[i]

<u>Finances</u>

England could no longer afford sustained military action in France. The territory held by the English in France had been a source of income for the English Crown, and the loss of regions like Normandy and southwest France deprived England of the revenue needed to finance military campaigns. A principal part of the English economy was the wool trade, and the war was harming it. Naval blockades and piracy were disrupting a steady flow of commercial traffic to the Continent.

England had imposed increasingly higher taxes on its population, which was causing internal problems. Direct taxes such as subsidies, which were taxes on normal goods and land, and poll taxes, which were flat-rate levies and a regressive tax, were becoming unbearable. These were in addition to taxes on imports and exports. By 1453, the English

---

[i] Britannica, E. o. (2024, August 1). *Hundred Years' War.* Retrieved from Britannica.com: https://www.britannica.com/event/Hundred-Years-War

Parliament was reluctant to approve even more taxes for the sake of continuing a war that the English were obviously losing.

Members of the royal court, including the duke of Suffolk, were accused of corruption and mismanagement of public funds. Although there is no specific evidence suggesting widespread mismanagement of public money, the cost of the war was oppressive, and the court's extravagance aroused suspicions.

Pressing Domestic Issues

There were domestic problems in England that sapped the will to continue aggressively fighting a foreign war. Taxation policies at unreasonably high tax rates led the peasants to extreme measures. Jack Cade's Rebellion of 1450 was an uprising in southeast England triggered by the abuse of power by local officials and King Henry's advisors. The Complaint of the Poor Commons of Kent was a manifesto that outlined the grievances of the common people. It demanded an inquiry into corruption at both the local and national levels. The high point of the insurrection was a march on London that caused an urban battle. Approximately 240 people were killed. It finally ended with the death of Jack Cade. There were other smaller uprisings in places such as Sussex, all of which were brought on by the poor administration of Henry's government.

A mural of Jack Cade's Rebellion.[34]

The Futility of the War

The defeat at Castillon and the loss of Bordeaux were signs of the declining military competence of the English forces abroad. The loss of critical territories cemented the belief that the war was no longer worth fighting. Desertions were becoming more frequent due to low morale and the inability to pay the troops. Nobody appeared willing to fight and die for a lost cause.

Unrest in the Ruling Class

The peasants were not the only people who were tired of fighting the French. The nobles also began losing interest in the war because it did not serve their personal interests.

Patriotism is something that has developed over the centuries, but in the 15th century, family and personal ambitions were more important. The English nobility supported the war effort primarily because they profited from it.

Feudal loyalty motivated nobles to fight, but there was also a motive for profit. Victory on the battlefield often resulted in barons being given grants of land and titles for their service. The income from rents and taxes increased the wealth of the English nobles. Furthermore, there were opportunities for making money by supplying troops with needed equipment or food. The estates that English nobles had in France were gradually lost, though. Their financial losses made English aristocrats question whether Henry VI should continue being the king.

A 16th-century portrait of Henry VI.[25]

The Rise of France

France did not need to pursue military operations against the English since Calais was the only territory the enemy had. It had the potential to be used as a launching point for military campaigns, but Calais was essentially a trading seaport. The English were too busy with their own internal affairs anyway. The French did not have much to worry about. In fact, France's chief priority in 1453 was the consolidation of the country and the creation of a centralized state.

Charles VII concentrated on consolidating royal power and creating a stable environment in France. His reforms gave France a reliable military and the tax revenue necessary to maintain that force.

The economy of France needed serious work, though. Charles appointed Jacques Coeur as master of the mint in 1436, and in the years that followed, Coeur improved coinage in France, making it a more dependable currency. He was also involved in several missions to the Middle East and created direct contacts that improved France's export trade.

Government reforms included re-establishing principal administrative services such as the Chancery, Parlement, and royal accounts in Paris. Government officials were replaced tactfully; there was no need for purges. Charles made important changes to how tax revenues were collected as well.[i]

Charles VII of France.[86]

Charles proved himself to be very adept at diplomacy. He used foreign relations effectively as a military strategy. The treaties of Arras and Tours are great examples of this. He eventually won the duke of Brittany over to his side, thereby eliminating a potential ally for England in future wars.

Impressive Social Changes

The economic recovery in France produced impressive results. Improvements in agriculture spurred productivity. The old practice of fallow land, where fields are not planted to allow them to recover from being used for farming, was being replaced by plain cover crops. Beans, turnips, and clover were some of the crops that were used to enrich the soil. High-value crops such as hops were cultivated as well.

---

[i] Bernard S. Bachrach, T. H. (2024, August 1). *Recovery and Reunification, 1429-83*. Retrieved from Britannica.com: https://www.britannica.com/place/France/Recovery-and-reunification-1429-83

The urban areas that had been hit by the war were reconstructed. It was more than just rebuilding fortifications, though. Public buildings and new infrastructure were being worked on as France was getting back on its feet. The guilds were becoming more robust, which meant that the quality standards and training of professionals improved.

France had been devastated by the Black Death and the Hundred Years' War. Stability permitted the population to grow, increasing the labor force. Charles put a lot of effort and time into turning his kingdom into the significant power it had once been. History shows he succeeded.

He did have problems with his son, the Dauphin, who would later rule as Louis XI. Louis was impatient to become the king, but when he finally was crowned, he continued to follow the sensible path of governance that his father had walked. France was more concerned with internal improvements than fighting senseless wars. If trouble flared up, Louis was more prone to use diplomacy instead of knights on horseback to resolve the issue.

<u>Consequences of Defeat</u>

A great controversy arose in the United States in the mid-20th century over who was responsible for China becoming a communist nation. While there was no "Who Lost France" movement in England, there is a strong argument that the conduct of the war contributed indirectly to the later Wars of the Roses.

England's setbacks and the rise of France underscored Henry VI's overall incompetence and his weak government. Henry was a well-meaning individual, but he was not a leader. His inability to make good decisions became increasingly apparent as time passed. The taxation required to maintain military campaigns abroad weakened the English economy and created substantial discontent among the people.[i]

A phenomenon arose during the 15th century in England later known as bastard feudalism. Essentially, bastard feudalism enabled the owners of large estates to call up hundreds of retainers to serve their lords in military service. This meant there were substantial private armies that owed only partial allegiance to the crown. The defeats in France and the end of major military campaigns meant there were English barons with private armies that could be used to pursue private interests. One noble

---

[i] Cartwright, M. (2020, February 12). *Causes of the Wars of the Roses.* Retrieved from Worldhistory.org: https://www.worldhistory.org/article/1498/causes-of-the-wars-of-the-roses/

who had a large military force behind him was Richard, Duke of York. He became so powerful that he began to have ambitions of taking the throne or at least being named the heir to Henry. His aspirations and those of other nobles who lost estates would eventually flare up into the Wars of the Roses.

The effective military campaigns of 1453 brought productive peace to one country and set the stage for anarchy in the other. The Hundred Years' War left behind a legacy that created monumental changes in Europe, spelled the end of the Middle Ages, and introduced a new and exciting epoch in European history.

Chapter 11: The Legacy

The Hundred Years' War was a time of violence and destruction. It was also an agent of change that left a legacy that endured for centuries. Innovation and creativity were as much a part of this epoch as the deaths incurred on the battlefields and in hospitals. Every segment of society was affected, and significant change occurred in some areas.

<u>Military Technology: Artillery and Gunpowder</u>

The longbow catches our imagination when we think of the Hundred Years' War. Archery, however, was always part of warfare; the composite bow of the Mongols was just as deadly as the English longbow. We have to admit that archery won major battles in the war, but it was artillery that eventually won it. Artillery in the 14th century was still a work in progress. Improvements were necessary to make this weapon effective, not just lethal. While the English continued to rely on archers, the French took the time and effort to create usable and accurate artillery.

It is well known that the Chinese invented gunpowder. They had hand cannons capable of firing projectiles and rockets, but gunpowder was commonly used for religious purposes and festivals. The English were using cannons as early as 1327. The French went further and fielded a large battery of cannons in the siege of Saint-Sauveur-le-Vicomte, an English stronghold in Normandy, in 1375. The guns they used weighed over a ton and could fire stone balls that weighed more than one hundred pounds.

Large artillery pieces, known as bombards, were manufactured by Burgundy in the 15th century. The early cannons were made of brass or copper and were later made from cast iron. The French continued to make improvements in the design of artillery. One type of cannon, the Veuglaire, was approximately eight feet long and weighed anywhere from 150 kilograms to several tons. Another French artillery piece, the crapaudine, was shorter and lighter.

The powder chamber of a Veuglaire.[i]

The French also developed effective tactics for using artillery. The placement of artillery at Formigny broke the English line and inflicted significant casualties.[i] At Castillon, the French used their cannon to destroy the walls of the English fortress and then used it to decimate the English force sent to relieve the siege.

The French use of artillery made the difference in several sieges. The walls of the English fortifications were not intended to resist artillery, so the curtain walls of many towns fell before the barrage of French cannons. The siege artillery used at Cherbourg caused the last English stronghold in Normandy to fall.

---

[i] 100-years-war.com. (2024, August 1). *The Battle of Formigny (1450)*. Retrieved from 100-years-war.com: https://www.100-years-war.com/the-battle-of-formigny

The blast furnace was a significant technological advance during the Hundred Years' War. Its ability to smelt large amounts of iron ore made casting artillery much easier and permitted the mass production of plate armor.

The End of Feudal Levies Provided Substantial Advantages

The traditional means of raising troops—feudal levies—disappeared during the Hundred Years' War. Professional standing armies began to appear, especially in France, and they offered substantial advantages. Standing armies received regular training and were more disciplined than feudal levied soldiers. Specialization was possible, meaning pikemen, archers, and cavalry were trained for particular combat roles. The soldiers of a standing army were not temporary fighters. They were permanent forces that could be used at any time. It was no longer necessary to go through mobilization efforts whenever danger arose. Professional soldiers could be rapidly deployed whenever needed.

Previously, soldiers were not regularly paid and relied on booty and pillage for compensation. The standing armies were paid on a routine basis and, thus, were more reliable. Rules of conduct were imposed on the troops to diminish the danger to noncombatants.

Mercenaries, notably the Swiss, would still be used in wars. However, the standing armies had a greater sense of patriotism and loyalty to the flag than paid foreigners. Their presence helped centralize political power. Kings could use their troops to enforce royal authority and uphold the laws.

In the early 14th century, feudalism was western Europe's primary political and social structure. It had been in place for centuries, and although it was not always just or reasonable, it gave stability to government and society. Feudalism was fading by the middle of the 15th century, though. The system gradually declined during the Hundred Years' War.

The cornerstone of feudalism was the protection that a local lord could give to the population. In exchange for relative security from banditry and pillaging, certain rights and privileges were granted. English chevauchées helped destroy that domestic protection. Local lords could not effectively stand up to several thousand mounted raiders who would pillage the country and then leave. It would take more than a baron and a few knights to provide protection. The royal government would be better able to respond to large incursions.

Soldiers from feudal levies could not be relied on. They were ordinarily raised for a given campaign, and then the men returned to their homes. Something more permanent was needed, which was why France ultimately turned to professional standing armies. Those men were recruited for careers in the military and could be depended upon to stay for several years or more.

The major casualty of the war was the use of chivalry. This code of conduct was almost dogma by the start of the conflict. However, by the end, the war had degenerated into an ugly affair in which chivalric behavior did not stand a chance. Tales of knights and their fair ladies were now relegated to the songs of troubadours and poets' rhymes.[i]

The Growth of the State

The standing professional armies required financing, which meant that taxation would have to be a regular occurrence. The king of France was not required to consult a legislative party about taxation policy, and the reforms of Charles VII created a tax system that brought a steady stream of revenue into the royal coffers. Taxes require a bureaucracy to collect and administer them. Charles was able to generate not only a standing army of soldiers but also an equally important army of bureaucrats who could oversee taxation and enforce any laws throughout the entire country, not just the area around Paris.

Taxation and bureaucracy served to consolidate power in the French monarchy. The king of France was now more powerful than before the Hundred Years' War, and this position of authority would endure until the French Revolution.

England would have to endure the chaos of the Wars of the Roses in the following years, which ultimately reduced the power of the nobility in England. The Tudor dynasty saw a resurgence of the monarchy, allowing a permanent administrative state in England to be formed. The Hundred Years' War also badly bruised the Roman Catholic Church, a powerbroker and social authority in the Middle Ages. Its weakened state left it vulnerable to the winds of change that finally started blowing in the 16th century.

---

[i] Cartwright, M. (2020, March 6). *The Hundred Years' War: Consequences & Effects.* Retrieved from Worldhistory.org: https://www.worldhistory.org/article/1520/the-hundred-years-war-consequences--effects/

The Great Equalizer

The Black Death brought about tremendous change in society. We know of the staggering mortality and the suffering the people endured during this pandemic, but historian Walter Scheidel argues that the Black Death had a leveling effect on society as well. Land ownership was very important before the pandemic, and serfs did not matter much. The Black Death reduced the value of land and increased the value of labor. The ruling class had to pay a premium for labor to harvest crops, which meant that the working class's living standards began to improve.

There were efforts to try to return to the status quo ante, notably in England, but living conditions gradually got better for surviving peasants. It was not just because of their ability to demand better wages. The feudal era required peasants to remain on traditional lands. Depopulation generated social mobility, which meant peasants could move about. The manorial system took a significant blow, and it never fully recovered. Land prices dropped, and people were able to buy property that had once been unaffordable. There were attempts to freeze wages, but the laws were not strictly enforced.

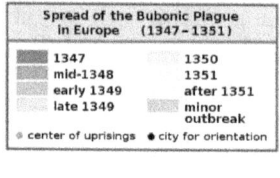

The spread of the Black Death in Europe (with modern borders drawn).[38]

The Hundred Years' War had a mixed impact on urban areas. Towns were destroyed by sieges, and the flight of people into the cities created overcrowding and social tensions. At the same time, the influx of people created a labor supply that helped increase the production of goods to be sold.

Nationalism

It was ordinary practice for people to consider themselves Normans or Yorkshire people. National identity was not of great importance. Something that the Hundred Years' War left for both France and England was a sense of national identity.

The development of nationalism came from many sources. National heroes came forward in the conflict. Joan of Arc is probably the most prominent. The Maid of Orléans inspired the French. Her leadership and martyrdom were stories that rallied the French to defend their country and drive out the English. King Henry V of England became a national hero for his victory at Agincourt. People celebrated with pride the military prowess of the English, especially that of the longbowmen who came from the common people.

Shared experiences also brought a sense of unity and cohesion. Whether recovering from devastating raids or being required to pay heavy taxes, popular movements rose up to demand that the government provide better services. France had to rebuild after the war, and this common effort to construct a new society helped bring people together.

The Arts

Thanks to Shakespeare's plays, we are reminded of the trauma of the Hundred Years' War. They tell the story of the tensions and hardships English people faced as defeat started to loom in the 15th century. Chaucer's *The Canterbury Tales* is still being read today. We have already mentioned Chaucer's impact on the mother tongue.

One of the most lasting legacies of the Hundred Years' War on England was the elevation of the English language. As national identity solidified, English replaced French in government, the law courts, and public life over the course of the 15th century. Language, once a marker of class division—French for the aristocracy, English for the peasantry—became a unifying force. By the end of the century, English had largely displaced French as the language of administration and culture. Though regional dialects persisted, English increasingly allowed people from different parts of the country to communicate more easily.

The Black Death fostered a very pessimistic environment. Artists tried to understand the damage and despair brought on by the disease. Death and mortality often influence realism in art. The *Danse Macabre*, which shows skeletons dancing close to living people, symbolizes the universality of death. Artistic scenes of dead bodies remind the viewer that life is fleeting and that death is a constant companion for everyone. An extraordinary example of the mortality theme is *Citizens of Tournai Bury Their Dead* by Pierart dou Tielt. The intense emotions and fear depicted in that work show a degree of naturalism that was uncommon in earlier artworks.

Citizens of Tournai Bury Their Dead.[39]

The death theme continued in Western art for centuries. The plague periodically struck Europe, although ordinarily in various regions instead of the entire continent. Artists such as Pieter Bruegel the Elder used dancing skeletons in the years to come to remind people of the triumph of death over humanity and that life was fleeting.[i]

---

[i] Anthony, J. (2023, October 6). *Black Death Art: Artistic Legacy of the Bubonic Plague.* Retrieved from artfilemagazine.com: https://artfilemagazine.com/black-death-art/

The Hundred Years' War was a catalyst for change in many areas of life. Stronger governments, nationalism, the development of a common language, and the influence of art shaped the consciousness of both nations. The war would not go quietly into the night. Instead, it left behind various reminders of what happened during that decades-old conflict.

Conclusion

The Hundred Years' War was a dramatic transition from the Middle Ages to the modern era. Medieval traditions and customs gave way to an energizing force coming out of Italy. There, the Renaissance was in full force. Humanism and reason took the place of strict dogma as the foundational stones of intellectualism. The Hundred Years' War disrupted the established social and political order. By doing so, it played a crucial role in creating a fertile ground for the Renaissance to flourish. Its impact is something we can all appreciate and learn from.

England would be distracted by the Wars of the Roses until 1487, but France was able to immediately benefit from the Renaissance. France would eventually become, once again, the dominant power in western Europe and would hold that title, with the exception of the late 16th and early 17th centuries when Spain was on top, well into the 18th century.

It would take years before Europe's population reached the numbers experienced before the Black Death. However, invention and experimentation with new procedures permitted western Europe to be productive. Constantinople fell at approximately the same time that hostilities ended in the Hundred Years' War. The new world that Christopher Columbus, a product of the post-war era, alerted Europe to would replace the eastern Mediterranean as a commercial opportunity. The resilience and adaptability of Europe after the war are a testament to its enduring strength and potential for growth.

The Hundred Years' War brought about a dramatic and brutal change in the conduct of wars. It marked a shift from local skirmishes fought by feudal levies to large standard armies engaging in long-distance battles. The war also saw the involvement of civilian populations and the transformation of cities into battlefields. This shift in warfare strategies, with its lasting impact on future conflicts, was a direct result of the Hundred Years' War, ensuring its enduring influence and making us aware of its historical significance.

The full significance of the Hundred Years' War is sometimes overshadowed by the Renaissance. However, the crucible of that conflict made the Renaissance more palatable. The war shattered the old social order, creating a blank slate upon which the incredible story of the Renaissance would be written. Europe was now poised to embark on an era of development and progress, the likes of which it had not seen for centuries.

There was a bothersome legacy of the war that lasted for centuries, but no one did anything about it. Finally, in 1802, with the Treaty of Amiens, the English monarchy formally renounced its claim to the French throne.

Here's another book by Enthralling History that you might like

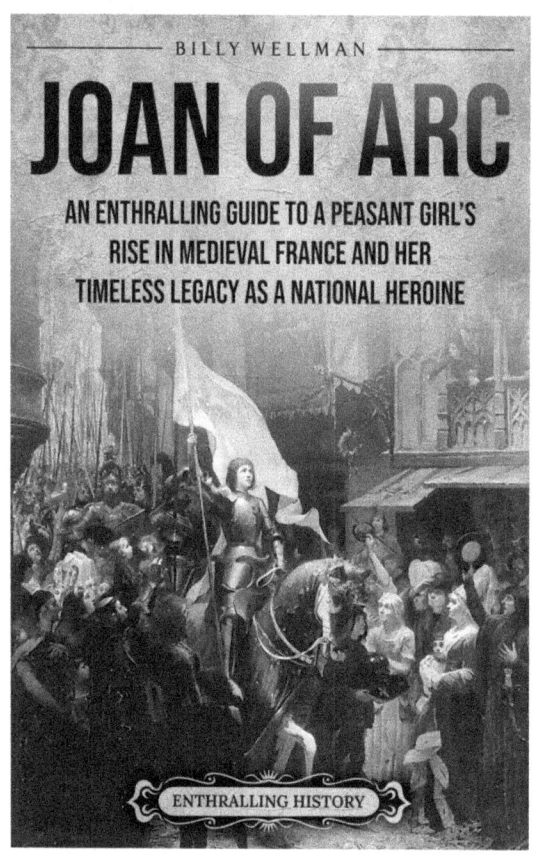

Free limited time bonus

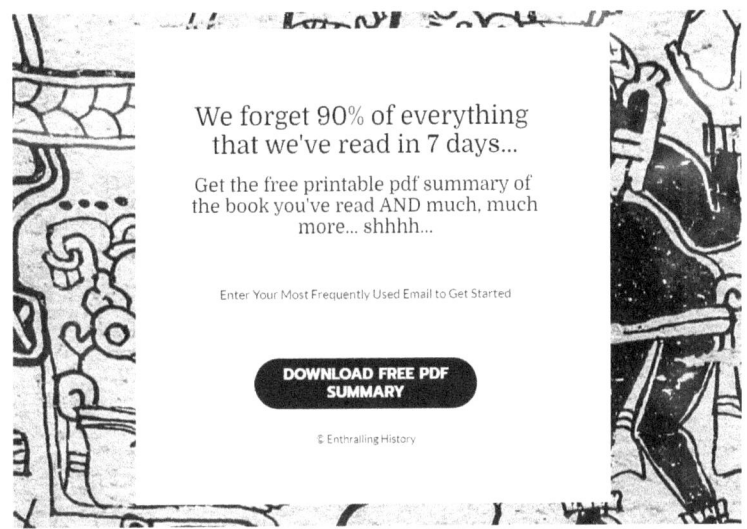

Stop for a moment. We have a free bonus set up for you. The problem is this: we forget 90% of everything that we read after 7 days. Crazy fact, right? Here's the solution: we've created a printable, 1-page pdf summary for this book that you're reading now. All you have to do to get your free pdf summary is to go to the following website:
https://livetolearn.lpages.co/enthrallinghistory/

Or, Scan the QR code!

Once you do, it will be intuitive. Enjoy, and thank you!

Bibliography

100-years-war.com. (2024, August 1). The Battle of Formigny (1450). Retrieved from 100-years-war.com: https://www.100-years-war.com/the-battle-of-formigny.

Adams, S. (2024, July 10). Battle of Poitiers. Retrieved from Britannica.com: https://www.britannica.com/event/Battle-of-Poitiers-French-history-1356.

Amelinckx, A. (2023, April 10). Joan of Arc's Tragic Final Words Before Her Executions. Retrieved from Grune.com: https://www.grunge.com/1246779/joan-of-arcs-tragic-final-words-before-her-execution/.

Anthony, J. (2023, October 6). Black Death Art: Artistic Legacy of the Bubonic Plague. Retrieved from artfilemagazine.com: https://artfilemagazine.com/black-death-art/.

BBC.co.uk. (2024, July 14). The Peasants' Revolt. Retrieved from BBC.co.uk: https://www.bbc.co.uk/bitesize/topics/z93txbk/articles/zyb77yc#zvrmm39.

Bernard S. Bachrach, T. H. (2024, August 1). Recovery and Reunification, 1429-83. Retrieved from Britannica.com: https://www.britannica.com/place/France/Recovery-and-reunification-1429-83.

Britannica, E. o. (2024, July 21). Charles VI. Retrieved from Britannica.com: https://www.britannica.com/biography/Charles-VI-king-of-France.

Britannica, E. o. (2024, July 30). Henry Beaufort. Retrieved from Britannica.com: https://www.britannica.com/biography/Henry-Beaufort.

Britannica, E. o. (2024, August 1). Hundred Years' War. Retrieved from Britannica.com: https://www.britannica.com/event/Hundred-Years-War.

Britannica, E. o. (2024, June 29). Philip VI. Retrieved from Britannica.com: https://www.britannica.com/biography/Philip-VI.

BritishBattles.com. (2024, July 7). Battle of Crecy. Retrieved from BritishBattles.com: https://www.britishbattles.com/one-hundred-years-war/battle-of-crecy/.

Britishbattles.com. (2024, July 10). Battle of La Rochelle. Retrieved from Britishbattles.com: https://www.britishbattles.com/one-hundred-years-war/battle-of-la-rochelle/.

Calhoun, D. B. (2012, December 4). John Wycliffe "The Morning Star of the Reformation." Retrieved from Cslewisinstitute.org: https://www.cslewisinstitute.org/resources/john-wycliffe-the-morning-star-of-the-reformation/.

Cartwright, M. (2020, March 2). Battle of Agincourt. Retrieved from Worldhistory.org: https://www.worldhistory.org/Battle_of_Agincourt/.

Cartwright, M. (2020, February 12). Causes of the Wars of the Roses. Retrieved from Worldhistory.org: https://www.worldhistory.org/article/1498/causes-of-the-wars-of-the-roses/.

Cartwright, M. (2020, March 6). The Hundred Years' War: Consequences & Effects. Retrieved from Worldhistory.org: https://www.worldhistory.org/article/1520/the-hundred-years-war-consequences--effects/.

Cartwright, M. (2023, April 5). Black Death. Retrieved from Worldhistory.org: https://www.worldhistory.org/Black_Death/.

Cole, M. (2020, August 9). How to Decipher the Symbolism in Jan Van Eyck's Famous "Arnolfini Portrait." Retrieved from Mymodernmet.com: https://mymodernmet.com/arnolfini-portrait/.

Couhlan, S. (2013, January 24). Medieval Warfare Had Well-Organized 'Ransom Market.'" Retrieved from BBC.com: https://www.bbc.com/news/education-21168437.

Cremer Consulting. (2019, July 8). Did Joan of Arc Suffer From Mental Illness? Retrieved from Cremerconsulting.com: https://www.cremerconsulting.com/en/did-joan-of-arc-suffer-from-mental-illness/.

Editors, H. (2018, August 21). Siege of Orleans. Retrieved from History.com: https://www.history.com/topics/middle-ages/siege-of-orleans.

Editors, H. (2023, March 28). Black Death. Retrieved from History.com: https://www.history.com/topics/middle-ages/black-death.

Encyclopedia.com. (2024, July 14). Avignon Papacy. Retrieved from Encyclopedia.com: https://www.encyclopedia.com/religion/encyclopedias-almanacs-transcripts-and-maps/avignon-papacy.

Focusonbelgium.be. (2015, October 13). Did You Know That Oil Painting Was Invented By the Belgian Van Eyck Brothers? Retrieved from

Focusonbelgium.be: https://focusonbelgium.be/en/facts/did-you-know-oil-painting-was-invented-belgian-van-eyck-brothers.

Frithowulf, H. (2023, November 9). Western Schism: The 14th Century Papal Schism. Retrieved from Malevus.com: https://malevus.com/western-schism/#how-did-the-western-schism-occur.

Gershon, L. (2023, August 18). Chivalry Was Established to Keep Thuggish Medieval Knights in Check. Retrieved from History.com: https://www.history.com/news/chivalry-knights-middle-ages.

Hayle, J. (2022, December 22). Accused: A Royal Witch in Medieval England. Retrieved from Hubpages.com: https://discover.hubpages.com/education/Eleanor-Duchess-of-Gloucester-Medieval-Royal-Accused-of-Witchcraft.

Hickman, K. (2019, September 3). Hundred Years' War. Retrieved from Thought.co: https://www.thoughtco.com/hundred-years-war-battle-of-crecy-2360728.

Hickman, K. (2020, March 2). Hundred Years' War: English Longbow. Retrieved from Thoughtco.com: https://www.thoughtco.com/hundred-years-war-english-longbow-2361241.

History Skills.com. (2024, July 10). Chevauchée: The Brutal War Tactics Knights Used to Terrorize the People of Medieval Europe. Retrieved from Historyskills.com: https://www.historyskills.com/classroom/year-8/chevauchée/.

History Skills.com. (2024, July 10). The Dramatic Battle of Poitiers: Where the Black Prince Captured the King of France. Retrieved from Historyskills.com: https://www.historyskills.com/classroom/year-8/battle-of-poitiers/.

History-maps.com. (2024, July 21). Treaty of Troyes. Retrieved from History-maps.com: https://history-maps.com/story/Hundred-Years-War/event/Treaty-of-Troyes.

HistoryTools.org. (2024, May 25). The Avignon Papacy: Popes, Politics, and Power in 14th Century Europe. Retrieved from HistoryTools.com: https://www.historytools.org/stories/the-avignon-papacy-popes-politics-and-power-in-14th-century-europe#google_vignette.

Hughes, T. (2019, March 11). What Were the Incidents of King Henry VI's Illness? Retrieved from Historyhit.com: https://www.historyhit.com/what-were-the-incidents-of-king-henry-vis-madness/.

II, A. L. (2024, June 29). Gascony and the Causes of the Hundred Years' War. Retrieved from Medievalists.net: https://www.medievalists.net/2020/02/gascony-causes-of-the-hundred-years-war/.

Internet Encyclopedia of Philosophy. (2024, June 29). Just War Theory. Retrieved from Iep.utm.edu: https://iep.utm.edu/justwar/.

Johnhus.org. (2023, February). Who Was John Hus? Retrieved from Johnhus.org: https://johnhus.org/content/who-was-jan-hus/.

Kiger, P. J. (2023, September 8). How the Black Death Spread Along the Silk Road. Retrieved from History.com: https://www.history.com/news/silk-road-black-death.

Kingscoronation.com. (2024, July 22). Coronation of Henry IV. Retrieved from Kingscoronation.com: https://kingscoronation.com/coronation-henry-iv/.

Knighton, A. (2016, September 6). A Force to Be Reckoned With: Mercenaries in the Hundred Years' War. Retrieved from Warhistoryonline.com: https://www.warhistoryonline.com/medieval/mercenaries-hundred-years-war.html.

Knighton, A. (2016, June 27). How Artillery Evolved in the 100 Years' War. Retrieved from Warhistoryonline.com: https://www.warhistoryonline.com/medieval/artillery-100-years-war.html.

Lanhers, Y. (2024, July 18). Charles VII. Retrieved from Britannica.com: https://www.britannica.com/biography/Charles-VII-king-of-France.

Libretexts.org. (2024, July 24). The Western Schism. Retrieved from Social.libretexts.org: https://socialsci.libretexts.org/Courses/Lumen_Learning/Book%3A_Western_Civilization_%28Lumen%29/Ch._08_The_Middle_Ages_in_Europe/09.8%3A_The_Western_Schism.

Lieberich, H. (2024, March 22). Louis IV. Retrieved from Britannica.com: https://www.britannica.com/biography/Louis-IV-Holy-Roman-emperor.

Longueville, O. (202, September 25). The Treaty of Arras of 1435: The End of the Civil Strife in France. Retrieved from Olivialongueville.com: https://olivialongueville.com/2020/09/25/the-treaty-of-arras-of-1435-the-end-of-the-civil-strife-in-france/.

Lumiansky, R. (2024, May 30). Geoffrey Chaucer Diplomat and Civil Servant. Retrieved from Britannica.com: https://www.britannica.com/biography/Geoffrey-Chaucer/Diplomat-and-civil-servant.

Mark, J. J. (2019, March 26). Christine de Pizan. Retrieved from Worldhistory.org: https://www.worldhistory.org/Christine_de_Pizan/.

Medieval Chronicles.com. (2024, July 10). "The Dark Side of Chivalry: Exploring the Brutal Realities of Medieval Combat." Retrieved from Medievalchronicles.com: https://www.medievalchronicles.com/medieval-life/code-of-chivalry/the-dark-side-of-chivalry-exploring-the-brutal-realities-of-medieval-combat/.

Medievalchronicles.com. (2024, July 10). A Brutal and Transformative Conflict: Exploring the Battles & Sieges of the Hundred Years' War. Retrieved from Medievalchronicles.com: https://www.medievalchronicles.com/medieval-battles-wars/a-brutal-and-transformative-conflict-exploring-the-battles-sieges-of-the-hundred-years-war/.

Medievalhistory.info. (2024, July 30). How England Lost the Hundred Years' War. Retrieved from Medievalhistory.info: https://medievalhistory.info/how-england-lost-the-hundred-years-war/.

Medievalhistory.info. (2024, July 30). The Treaty of Tours-Peace in Our Time. Retrieved from Medievalhistory.info: https://medievalhistory.info/the-treaty-of-tours-peace-in-out-time-1444/.

Miller, S. G. (2016, July 29). What Really Caused the Voices in Joan of Arc's Head? Retrieved from Livescience.com: https://www.livescience.com/55597-joan-of-arc-voices-epilepsy.html.

Moorhouse, D. (2022, May 20). French Raid on Plymouth. Retrieved from Thehundredyearswar.com: https://thehundredyearswar.co.uk/french-raid-on-plymouth/.

MSW. (2009, February 9). Naval Warfare in the 100 Years' War. Retrieved from Weaponsandwarfare.com: https://weaponsandwarfare.com/2009/02/10/naval-warfare-in-the-100-years-war/#google_vignette.

New World Encyclopedia. (2024, July 10). Battle of Poitiers. Retrieved from New World Encyclopedia.org: https://www.newworldencyclopedia.org/entry/Battle_of_Poitiers.

New World Encyclopedia.org. (2024, July 19). Charles VI of France. Retrieved from Newworldencyclopedia.org: https://www.newworldencyclopedia.org/entry/Charles_VI_of_France.

Palais-des-papes.com. (2024, July 22). Priceless Frescoes. Retrieved from Palais-des-papes.com: https://palais-des-papes.com/des-fresques-inestimables/.

Poets.org. (2024, July 22). Geoffrey Chaucer. Retrieved from Poets.org: https://poets.org/poet/geoffrey-chaucer.

PopeHistory.com. (2024, July 14). Pope Martin V. Retrieved from PopeHistory.com: https://popehistory.com/popes/pope-martin-v/.

Rosen, M. (2021, July 14). The History Behind Shakespeare's Henriad Series. Retrieved from Leoweekly.com.

Sargent, F. (2018). The Wine Trade with Gascony. Retrieved from British History Online: https://www.british-history.ac.uk/manchester-uni/london-lay-subsidy/1332/pp256-311.

Saul, N. (2011, 02 17). Richard II and the Crisis of Authority. Retrieved from BBC.co.uk: https://www.bbc.co.uk/history/british/middle_ages/richardii_crisis_01.shtml.

Shakespeare, W. (2024, July 10). Henry V-3.3.1. Retrieved from Folger.edu: https://www.folger.edu/search/?q=Harfleur&area=works&work=henry-v.

Solly, M. (2019, October 31). The True Story of Henry V, England's Warrior King. Retrieved from Smithsonianmag.org: https://www.smithsonianmag.com/history/true-story-henry-v-englands-warrior-king-180973432/.

Sotonopedia.wikidot.com. (2024, July 7). French Raid. Retrieved from Sotonopedia.wikidot.com: http://sotonopedia.wikidot.com/page-browse:french-raid.

Spottinghistory.com. (2024, July 22). Palais des Papes. Retrieved from Spottinghistory.com: https://www.spottinghistory.com/view/6387/palais-des-papes/.

Strachan, D. (2024, July 22). La Lingua Toscana: Tuscany's Dialect and the Birth of Italian. Retrieved from Tuscanynowandmre.com: https://www.tuscanynowandmore.com/discover-italy/history/italian-language-tuscan-dialect.

The Scottish History Society. (2024, June 29). The Wars of Independence. Retrieved from Scottishhistorysociety.com: https://scottishhistorysociety.com/the-wars-of-independence/.

Theartstory.org. (2024, July 22). Summary of Jan Van Eyck. Retrieved from Theartstory.org: https://www.theartstory.org/artist/van-eyck-jan/.

University of California Press. (2024, June 29). The Five Substitutions. Retrieved from UC Press E-Books Collection, 1982-2004: https://publishing.cdlib.org/ucpressebooks/view?docId=ft8k4008jd&chunk.id=d0e4248&toc.depth=1&toc.id=d0e4231&brand=ucpress#:~:text=When%20Philip%20of%20Valois%20came,fidelity%20to%20the%20French%20ruler.

Valjak, D. (2017, March 3). Pope Clement VI: The Generous and Progressive Pope Who Granted Remission of Sins to All People Who Died of the Plague. Retrieved from Thevintagenews.com: https://www.thevintagenews.com/2017/03/03/pope-clement-vi-the-generous-and-progressive-pope-who-granted-remission-of-sins-to-all-people-who-died-of-the-plague/.

Vioux, M. (2024, July 19). Rivalry with Charles V. Retrieved from Britannica.com: https://www.britannica.com/biography/Francis-I-king-of-France/Rivalry-with-Charles-V.

Whelan, E. (2020, February 18). English Medieval Hospital Shows Horrors of Black Death. Retrieved from Ancient-origins.net: https://www.ancient-origins.net/news-history-archaeology/black-death-0013302.

Wisse, J. (2002, October). Burgundian Netherlands: Private Life. Retrieved from Metmuseum.org: https://www.metmuseum.org/toah/hd/bnpr/hd_bnpr.htm.

Worldhistory.edu. (2024, February 5). What Transpired at the Battle of Shrewsbury in 1403. Retrieved from Worldhistory.edu: https://worldhistoryedu.com/what-transpired-at-the-battle-of-shrewsbury-in-1403/.

Yvonne Lanhers, M. G. (2024, June 5). St. Joan of Arc. Retrieved from Britannica.com: https://www.britannica.com/biography/Saint-Joan-of-Arc.

Image Sources

1 https://commons.wikimedia.org/wiki/File:King_Edward_III_from_NPG.jpg
2 https://commons.wikimedia.org/wiki/File:BattleofSluys.jpeg
3 https://commons.wikimedia.org/wiki/File:Siege_of_Limoges.jpg
4 https://commons.wikimedia.org/wiki/File:Edward_the_Black_Prince_1430.jpg
5 https://commons.wikimedia.org/wiki/File:Jean_Froissart,_Chroniques,_154v,_12148_btv1b8438605hf336,_crop.jpg
6 https://commons.wikimedia.org/wiki/File:Map-_France_at_the_Treaty_of_Bretigny.jpg
7 https://commons.wikimedia.org/wiki/File:Johnofgaunt.jpg
8 https://commons.wikimedia.org/wiki/File:A_Chronicle_of_England_-_Page_328_-_Arundel,_Gloucester,_Nottingham,_Derby,_and_Warwick,_Before_the_King.jpg
9 Reigen, CC BY-SA 4.0 <https://creativecommons.org/licenses/by-sa/4.0>, via Wikimedia Commons, https://commons.wikimedia.org/wiki/File:Reconquest_Charles_V.svg
10 https://commons.wikimedia.org/wiki/File:Mort_de_Bertrand_Du_Guesclin.jpg
11 https://commons.wikimedia.org/wiki/File:Henry_V_Miniature.jpg
12 https://commons.wikimedia.org/wiki/File:Joan_of_Arc_miniature_graded.jpg
13 https://commons.wikimedia.org/wiki/File:The_Arnolfini_portrait_(1434).jpg
14 https://commons.wikimedia.org/wiki/File:Portrait_of_a_Man_by_Jan_van_Eyck-small.jpg
15 Diliff, CC BY-SA 3.0 <https://creativecommons.org/licenses/by-sa/3.0>, via Wikimedia Commons, https://commons.wikimedia.org/wiki/File:York_Minster_Chapter_House,_Nth_Yorkshire,_UK_-_Diliff.jpg

16 François de Dijon, CC BY-SA 3.0 <https://creativecommons.org/licenses/by-sa/3.0>, via Wikimedia Commons, https://commons.wikimedia.org/wiki/File:Avignon_Palais_des_Papes_2013.jpg

17 https://commons.wikimedia.org/wiki/File:Vigiles_du_roi_Charles_VII_42.jpg

18 Diliff, CC BY-SA 3.0 <https://creativecommons.org/licenses/by-sa/3.0>, via Wikimedia Commons, https://commons.wikimedia.org/wiki/File: Duke_Humfrey%27s_Library_Interior_5,_Bodleian_Library,_Oxford,_UK_-_Diliff.jpg

19 Charles Heath, CC0, via Wikimedia Commons, https://commons.wikimedia.org/wiki/File:Suffolk_and_Margaret_(Shakespeare,_King_Henry_VI,_Part_I,_Act_5,_Scene_3)_MET_DP870115.jpg

20 https://commons.wikimedia.org/wiki/File:1436_Entr%C3%A9e_Paris.jpg

21 PHGCOM, CC BY-SA 4.0 <https://creativecommons.org/licenses/by-sa/4.0>, via Wikimedia Commons, https://commons.wikimedia.org/wiki/File: HandCulverinWithSmallCannonsEurope15thCentury.jpg

22 https://commons.wikimedia.org/wiki/File:Vigiles_de_ Charles_VII,_fol._205,_Si%C3%A8ge_de_Cherbourg_(1450).jpg

23 https://commons.wikimedia.org/wiki/File:Fran%C3%A7ais_5054,_ fol._229v,_Bataille_de_Castillon_1453_-_d%C3%A9tail.jpg

24 Paul Simpson from London, England, CC BY 2.0 <https://creativecommons.org/licenses/by/2.0>, via Wikimedia Commons, https://commons.wikimedia.org/wiki/File:The_History_of_the_Old_Kent_Road_-_7_(2793392566).jpg

25 https://commons.wikimedia.org/wiki/File:King_Henry_VI_from_NPG_(2).jpg

26 https://commons.wikimedia.org/wiki/File:KarlVII.jpg

27 https://commons.wikimedia.org/wiki/File:Veuglaire_powder_box_ caliber_130_length_107_early_15th_century_La_Fere.jpg

28 Original by Roger Zenner (de-WP)Enlarging & readability editing by user Jaybear, CC BY-SA 3.0 <http://creativecommons.org/licenses/by-sa/3.0/>, via Wikimedia Commons, https://commons.wikimedia.org/wiki/File:Bubonic_plague_map.PNG

29 https://commons.wikimedia.org/wiki/File:Burying_Plague_Victims_of_Tournai.jpg

www.ingramcontent.com/pod-product-compliance
Lightning Source LLC
Chambersburg PA
CBHW070335010526
44107CB00004B/515